Easy Mind-Reading Tricks

ROBERT MANDELBERG

Illustrated by
Ferruccio Sardella

Sterling Publishing Co., Inc.
New York

To my two girls.

A special thanks to Rodman and Ferruccio.

OTHER BOOKS BY ROBERT MANDELBERG
Mind-Reading Card Tricks
The Case of the Curious Campaign:
A Whodunit of Many Mini-Mysteries
Mystifying Mind Reading Tricks

Author's Photograph: S. Keith Rosenthal (p. 96)
Diagram Art: Robert Steimle (pp. 27, 47, 48, 83)
Editor and Layout: Rodman Pilgrim Neumann

Library of Congress Cataloging-in-Publication Data

Mandelberg, Robert.
  Easy mind-reading tricks / Robert Mandelberg ; illustrated by Ferruccio Sardella.
    p. cm.
  Includes index.
  ISBN 1-4027-2164-1
  1. Magic tricks. 2. Telepathy. I. Title.

GV1553.M33 2005
793.8--dc22

                                             2005002257

2 4 6 8 10 9 7 5 3 1
Published by Sterling Publishing Co., Inc.
387 Park Avenue South, New York, NY 10016
© 2005 by Robert Mandelberg
Distributed in Canada by Sterling Publishing
C/o Canadian Manda Group, One Atlantic Avenue, Suite 105
Toronto, Ontario, Canada M6K 3E7
Distributed in Great Britain by Chrysalis Books Group PLC
The Chrysalis Building, Bramley Road, London W10 6SP, England
Distributed in Australia by Capricorn Link (Australia) Pty. Ltd.
P.O. Box 704, Windsor, NSW 2756 Australia

Sterling ISBN 1-4027-2164-1

For information about custom editions, special sales, premium
and corporate purchases, please contact Sterling Special Sales
Department at 800-805-5489 or specialsales@sterlingpub.com.

Contents

*I*ntroduction

When will we learn to stop stereotyping people? Most people think of mind readers as creepy lunatics who wear dark capes, spooky eye patches, and oversized clown shoes. I am saddened when I hear these distortions. The truth is that my clown shoes fit me perfectly.

The fact that you are holding this book in your hand leads me to believe that you would like to join the ranks of us eye-patch-wearing outcasts. If so, I feel that it is my obligation to alert you to the darker side of this avocation.

Contrary to popular belief, mind reading is not all glamour and excitement. Oh, sure, we get to deceive our closest friends and watch them recoil in terror as we seemingly steal the thoughts out of their very brains, but there's also a negative aspect that you may not have considered.

Once you dazzle your friends, family, and acquaintances with a series of devastating, mind-blowing psychic feats, they will forever hound you until you agree to an encore. Your private life will cease to exist. Wherever you go, you will be pursued, pestered, and plagued by people who yearn to see you *do that again!* Does this sound like any life worth living?

I realize, of course, that the desire to read minds is so alluring that you may foolishly decide to ignore my advice and read through the rest of this book. If this is the case, then

5

you will soon learn some of the most powerful and closely guarded secrets in mentalism. You will be equipped with an arsenal of stunning and devastating mind-reading tricks that you can unleash on audiences large and small.

Please understand that once you start the next page, there's no turning back. The existence you have known up until now will be changed forever. And if my words of warning are not convincing enough to sway you away from this endeavor, then I strongly recommend that you purchase a disguise so that you can maintain some semblance of a private life. May I suggest a dark cape, a spooky eye patch, and clown shoes?

— Robert Mandelberg

Mind Reading, Philosophy & Rating System

In addition to revealing the secrets to 16 blockbuster mind-reading demonstrations, I have also provided ratings for each trick (is there no end to my kindness?). So whether you are seeking a quick and simple stunt to perform for your family, friends, and parole officer—or you're looking for a more powerful demonstration for larger groups—the rating system will help you determine which entries are right for you.

You can also use the ratings to build an entertaining mind-reading repertoire. Start by loosening up your audience with an ice-breaker, bewilder them with a few dazzling feats of mentalism, and then finish them off with an earth-shattering psychic miracle that sends them running into the street screaming in terror.

When judging whether or not to include a trick in your routine, ask yourself three questions:

- Does the trick have a powerful impact?
- Is the trick easy to perform?
- Is there a low risk of getting caught?

Wouldn't it be great if you could find a trick that gives you "yes" answers to all three questions? Unfortunately, perfect tricks are rare and mind readers generally have to decide which elements are most important to them. Most tricks will often render "yes" answers to only two out of the three questions.

In general, you will find that the following holds true:

Easy trick + powerful impact = high risk
Easy trick + small risk = low impact
Powerful impact + low risk = high level of difficulty

But isn't that true with everything in life? Those things that are worth doing usually require effort and carry with them a certain level of risk. See what just happened? You bought a book on mind reading and you got a little philosophy thrown in (at no extra charge!).

And like everything in life, each mind-reading trick has varying degrees of difficulty, impact, and risk. The focus of this book is on mind-reading tricks that are easy to master and perform. For this collection, I have researched, selected, improved, or invented some of the **very best** easy psychic feats ever created. Not only have I described the tricks, but I have also included numerous insider tips, performance suggestions, and creative hints to help you *maximize the impact* and *minimize the risk*. I do not, however, provide this same type of advice for life. You're on your own there.

Rating System

Each entry in this collection is simple enough for you to perform, yet powerful enough to impress and entertain even the most skeptical audiences. I've rated each trick for impact, difficulty, and risk to help you compile a routine that suits your needs. Let's take a closer look at each of these categories:

DIFFICULTY LEVEL: ✦✦✦✦✦
Because this book is dedicated to easy mental magic, none of these entries has a difficulty rating higher than three. This doesn't mean that the demonstrations I've listed will perform themselves; you have to put in a little effort to make the tricks work. If you see a rating of ✦✦✦✦✦, you will most likely be able to perform the trick blindfolded (and in some of the tricks you *will be* blindfolded!).

A rating of ✦✦✦✦✦, however, means that the trick is more challenging and will require some work on your part. These selections are usually of higher quality and have a much greater impact on the audience. Demonstrations with this rating are generally more involved and feature many steps. But don't worry! None of these steps require complicated moves, fancy sleight of hand maneuvers, or complex codes. If a trick calls for you to make a switch, it will be an easy move that you can master with a little practice.

IMPACT: ✳✳✳✳✳

Probably the most important element of a trick is it's impact. You need to ask yourself: *Is this trick worth performing?* Will my audience be impressed and entertained? In this collection, the answer to that question will always be *yes!* Even some of the simpler tricks that I recommend using as a warm-up are extremely fun to perform and witness.

In this category, if you see a low ranking (✳✳✳ ✳ ✳), consider using the trick as an ice-breaker. Even though the impact may be low, you will find that you can still transform it into a blockbuster with the proper presentation. But when you see a high rating (✳✳✳✳✳ or ✳✳✳✳✳✳), be prepared for some wild reactions from the audience. With these high-impact tricks, it may be a good idea to have smelling salts available and a physician standing by, as some of your spectators may need to be revived afterwards.

RISK: ✔✔✔✔✔

Here is the category that seems to be at the forefront of every psychic's mind. *What is the risk of getting caught?* I understand completely. No one wants to be seen pulling a fast one in front of a group of friends—or even worse, strangers!

Let's face it: Every mind-reading exhibition carries some degree of risk. For a trick to be effective, you're going to have to do something sneaky—whether it's presetting a deck of cards, or switching envelopes, or employing a secret code, or even using mathematics to fool your audience (more on these techniques later).

As much as we would like there to be foolproof tricks, there is almost always *a chance* of getting caught. Some risks are greater than others—but then so, too, are the payoffs. Would it be worth it to take a slightly larger risk of getting caught if it meant that you could leave your audience stupefied and yanking their hair out of their heads? For those of you who have ever witnessed a person yanking hair out of his head, the answer is clear.

As you read these demonstrations, I ask you to *trust me!* If you follow each explanation through to the end, you will see that I have left no stone unturned in accounting for possible pitfalls. You will find techniques to minimize the risk through carefully timed switches, misdirection, and other distractions. I will alert you to recognize which parts of the tricks are the riskiest and I will provide options to overcome potential obstacles.

As a brief reference, here is a key to the rating system used in the book:

DIFFICULTY LEVEL

◆◆◆◆◆ (Do not try this at home! Houdini himself would have trouble)

◆◆◆◆◇ (Very challenging—only for skilled or practiced magicians)

◆◆◆◇◇ (Requires some practice)

◆◆◇◇◇ (Piece of cake)

◆◇◇◇◇ (No challenge at all)

IMPACT

✳✳✳✳✳ (Jaw-dropping, hair-standing-up-on-end, screaming-in-the-street amazing)

✳✳✳✳✳ (Shocking!)

✳✳✳✳✳ (Fun and baffling)

✳✳✳✳✳ (Use as a warm-up)

✳✳✳✳✳ (Snoozer)

RISK

✔✔✔✔✔ (Yikes! Very risky! Run for the hills!)

✔✔✔✔✔ (Be very careful—considerable risk involved)

✔✔✔✔✔ (Use caution)

✔✔✔✔✔ (Nothing to worry about)

✔✔✔✔✔ (Practically risk-free)

Technique

Let me start off by doling out some bad news: If you were hoping that I was going to teach you how to read someone's mind by casting a spell or brewing a magic elixir, you're about to be gravely disappointed. The truth is that in order for you to create the illusion that you can read minds, you're going to have to be sneaky: Lie, mislead, and con your audience to trick them into thinking that you possess supernatural psychic abilities.

Oh, is your conscience acting up at the thought of deceiving people? Here's my advice: Whenever you hear that little voice in your head (you do hear little voices in your head, don't you?) start to whine about decency and morals, do what I do—ignore it. When faced with a choice of acting ethically or being sneaky and freaking out a group of people you love and respect, take the low road—you'll thank me for it.

Once you get a taste of how it feels to pull off an impossible mind-reading stunt, you will quickly become addicted. The look of disbelief and bewilderment on the faces of your audience will surely outweigh those small pangs of guilt you may experience from a few little white lies. Oh, and just wait until you see how easy it is to do it!

Professional mentalists go to incredible lengths to create the illusion that they can read minds. From elaborate contraptions to using audience "stooges" to concealing complex surveillance equipment, psychic performers have devised the most innovative methods to bamboozle their audiences. Not to worry! In *Easy Mind-Reading Tricks,* we will stay away from anything that requires a degree in electronics engineering or expertise in military intelligence.

With few exceptions, the tricks in this book require only basic props: a deck of cards, some paper, pens, napkins, and envelopes. There is one trick that calls for a small blackboard and a piece of chalk. If you decide that you'd like to use that trick, you can pick up these supplies at most discount stores.

In reading through the upcoming chapters, you will notice that most of the demonstrations I describe fall into one of several categories:

Mind Reading

To mind-reading aficionados, this is mentalism in its purest sense. The subject thinks of a word, number, question, or fact of his own choosing (ha!), and the mind reader is able to figure out what it is. Another common method of mind reading is having a subject randomly (again, ha!) arrive at a number or playing card or even a name in the telephone book. The mind reader then telepathically determines what it is. It is the illusion of randomness that makes these tricks so startling—and so effective.

Thought Control

These demonstrations are rather striking and memorable because they appear as if the mentalist had actually planted thoughts into the heads of his subjects. But we all know that this is impossible . . . don't we?

Predictions

The most remarkable demonstrations are usually those where the performer predicts something that a subject will say or choose.

A common way that this method is used is for the performer to seal his prediction in an envelope and give it to an audience member for safekeeping. After the subject announces his randomly chosen name, date, card, etc., the envelope is opened to reveal a perfect match with the mind reader's prediction.

To keep your audience mesmerized and entertained, I recommend that you learn a few demonstrations in each category.

Once you have proven that you can predict future events, move on to other styles. Mixing up the demonstrations will showcase your versatility and add to the entertainment value of your performance.

Mind reading, thought control, and predictions all sound like remarkable feats, but how can they be accomplished? Voodoo dolls? Crystal balls? Regular exercise and three balanced meals a day? Well, except for the last suggestion, none of these ideas will have the slightest impact on your ability to perform top-notch psychic stunts. You will have to use cunning, intuition, ingenuity, and a liberal dose of sneakiness and deception to fool your audiences. If you are only beginning to explore the art of mind reading, you will be impressed by the ingenius methods used to dupe audiences. Let's take a look at some of the techniques you'll be learning in this book:

SWITCHING

As you will soon see, "switching" is one of my favorite methods. In several of the upcoming demonstrations, I will describe how you can achieve startling results by performing simple (but oh-so-sneaky) switching maneuvers. In many cases, you will be switching envelopes, or cards, or slips of paper—and, in one really amazing trick, little napkin balls. And what do you switch them with? Usually identical envelopes or papers that contain "predictions" that you prepared ahead of time.

I will teach you to use misdirection and sensible preplanning to distract your audience so that you can safely execute the switches. Most of the time, these will be low-risk moves that you can master with a little practice.

MATHEMATICS

For most of us, mathematics is a handy tool that we use often to help us make our lives easier. But wait until you see what has happened to it! Thought readers have transformed the ancient science of math into a tool for deceit and trickery.

Math tricks are often the safest to perform. This is because the math does all the work for you. There's nothing to hide, switch, fake, or alter. Once you set the trick in motion, math takes over and helps you create a dazzling illusion of telepathy.

Partner & Code

Although I enjoy using a partner quite extensively when performing mind-reading exhibitions, I realize that a lot of people prefer working alone. In this collection, I describe only one trick that requires a partner. Acute Senses uses an extremely simple code that you can learn in less than a minute. The presentation is so much fun that I couldn't resist including it. It's also great to use in combination with other demonstrations.

Sleight of Hand

Normally a very sophisticated and complex technique used in mind reading, sleight of hand maneuvers can help produce some unfathomable miracles. But not to worry! The moves that you will learn in this book are simple, low-risk, and, in some cases, not at all painful.

One-Ahead Principle

Ah, what can I say about the most brilliant and mind-blowing thought-reading technique ever invented? No collection would be complete without an example of the one-ahead method. The trick entitled Little Napkin Balls is an excellent example of how you can perform miracles by staying "one ahead" of your audience.

Finger Crossing

Yes, finger crossing—old-fashioned, hold-your-breath, cross-your-fingers, and hope that everything works out perfectly. You see, there are two tricks in this collection where I will be asking you to rely on spectators to secretly help you pull a fast one on your audience. And since you can never tell how a spectator will react, I strongly suggest that you cross those fingers for good luck! Actually, it's not as bad as it sounds. If performed correctly, these tricks are usually among the most memorable of the evening.

$\mathcal{P}$erformance & $\mathcal{E}$xecution

Now that you have a collection of quality mind-reading demonstrations, it will be up to you to make sure that they are performed correctly. Each chapter is filled with myriad suggestions to help you execute the tricks flawlessly. From introducing the premise to presenting the conclusion, you will learn everything you need to know to overcome performance obstacles and increase your chances of success. Some of the trickier moves may require a little practice on your end, but it will be well worth it.

In many of the demonstrations that follow, you will notice that the purpose of the trick is hidden until the end. This adds a sense of intrigue and suspense to the demonstration, and it steers the audience off the trail. Keep them in the dark as long as possible and it will be easier for you to pull a fast one—since your audience will not know where they should be looking to catch you doing that sneaky thing you're about to do. Sure, they see one spectator holding a book and another guarding an envelope and yet another writing down numbers, but they do not know *why*; nor do they know the relationships among all of the elements. This allows you to present a spectacular and unexpected conclusion to your trick.

Presentation

Presentation is every bit as important as execution. Many beginners make the mistake of ignoring the creative part of the demonstration and go straight for the kill. What's the rush? *The trick is going to work.* There is no need to race toward the finish. I understand that it is exciting when you realize that you've gotten away

15

with something very sneaky and are about to put your audience in a state of shock, but I implore you to take your time; savor the moment. Tease the audience by prolonging the finale; make them wait until you are good and ready to bring it to its conclusion.

My favorite part of thought reading is the performance and showmanship behind each demonstration. In the coming pages you will see in-depth, top-notch performance ideas for each trick. Of course, these are merely suggestions; feel free to use your own creativity to personalize the selections.

My point is that you can turn an ordinary trick into a highly entertaining, suspenseful feat of mentalism with a little showmanship. Don't be afraid to dream up outrageous stories or perform bizarre stunts if it will add to the overall effect. What style is right for you? You'll have to experiment until you find the best mood and approach to fit your personality. Familiarize yourself with several performance techniques so that you will be prepared for any occasion.

As a final note, I'd like to mention the importance of guarding these secrets closely. You will find that this is not always easy to do. When your audience sees you perform a particularly incredible mind-reading exhibition they will insist upon knowing the solution. And what do I mean by insist? Let me put it this way: Do not be surprised if you see a few spectators crawling by your feet, tugging on your pant leg, pleading to know your secrets. I realize that witnessing this pathetic sight might tempt you to weaken and tell all, but I warn you—don't! Because once you reveal the solution, these begging, pleading, wretched souls who are whimpering and clinging to your cuffs will instantly transform into arrogant know-it-alls who somehow "knew it all the time." Take it from me: Take your bows and keep silent! You'll be glad you did.

I hope that you enjoy performing these psychic feats as much as I have over the years. If you would like to learn more incredible mind-reading stunts, my other books, *Mystifying Mind Reading Tricks* and *Mind-Reading Card Tricks,* feature a wide variety of high-impact and entertaining demonstrations.

Are you ready to begin your journey? Take a deep breath, keep an open mind, and enjoy your plunge into the depths of the mysterious art of mind reading.

The Power of Nine

3

DIFFICULTY LEVEL: ◆ ◆ ◆ ◆ ◆
IMPACT: ✱ ✱ ✱ ✱ ✱
TECHNIQUE: MATHEMATICS
RISK: ✔ ✔ ✔ ✔ ✔

Overview

From as far back as the Ancient Greek civilization, the number nine has been regarded as a mystical and sacred symbol, possessing great powers and significance. What does that have to do with mind reading? Nothing at all, but it makes for great banter as you are performing the next two tricks.

For those interested in mathematics, you may have already discovered the brilliance of the number nine. This remarkable digit is often at the center of perplexing mathematical oddities. As you will see in the first two demonstrations, all roads lead to nine.

Let's start off with the most popular number nine trick ever invented. Variations of this trick have been circulating over the Internet for the past several years. I will now present my favorite version. Be sure to check Tips & Techniques for some original and entertaining ways to present the conclusion.

Premise

The mind reader asks a spectator to perform a series of simple mathematical tasks followed by several easy questions. Although the spectator makes her choices freely, the mind reader is able to predict every selection.

The spectator is asked to do the following (try it yourself as you read along):

Step 1: Pick a number between 1 and 10.

Step 2: Multiply that number by 9.

Step 3: Now you have a two-digit number. Add those numbers together.

Step 4: From that total, subtract 5.

With me so far?

Step 5: Take that number and find its corresponding letter. What do I mean by that? This is easy:

1 = A
2 = B
3 = C
4 = D
5 = E

And so forth. Hang in there; we're almost done.

Step 6: Now think of a country that begins with that letter.

Step 7: Think of the LAST letter of that country. Now think of an animal that starts with that letter.

Step 8. Think of the LAST letter of that animal. Now think of a fruit that starts with that letter.

Got it?

Okay. Are you, perchance, possibly, perhaps thinking of . . .

A kangaroo eating an orange in Denmark?

Yes? Well, you're not alone! Read on to find out why.

Solution

It is the Power of Nine that lies behind the answer to this fun little exhibition. After you take a closer look at the first part of this trick, the solution will become clear. A spectator is asked to think of a number between 1 and 10. For the sake of this explanation, let's assume that she selected 3 as her number.

In the next step, the spectator is asked to multiply her number by 9. For those of you unfamiliar with the "new math," allow me to help you along.

9 x 3 = 27

18

Next, the spectator is required to add these numbers together:

$2 + 7 = 9$

And there's the answer. You see, no matter what number the spectator selects (between 1 and 10), when she multiplies it by 9, the two digits will *always* add up to 9. Don't believe me? Check it out:

$$2 \times 9 = 18 \text{ and } 1 + 8 = 9$$
$$3 \times 9 = 27 \text{ and } 2 + 7 = 9$$
$$4 \times 9 = 36 \text{ and } 3 + 6 = 9$$
$$5 \times 9 = 45 \text{ and } 4 + 5 = 9$$
$$6 \times 9 = 54 \text{ and } 5 + 4 = 9$$
$$7 \times 9 = 63 \text{ and } 6 + 3 = 9$$
$$8 \times 9 = 72 \text{ and } 7 + 2 = 9$$
$$9 \times 9 = 81 \text{ and } 8 + 1 = 9$$
$$10 \times 9 = 90 \text{ and } 9 + 0 = 9$$

Technically, 1 is not "between" 1 and 9; but if the participant selects 1, the trick will still work (there will only be one digit to add: $9 + 0 = 9$).

Although the spectator thinks that she has free choice to select a random number, she will always end up with 9 in the third step of this trick. Knowing this, you will ask the spectator to subtract 5 from her number. As you can see, there's no way around it. Every time the trick is performed, the spectator will *always* wind up with the number 4 at this point. The rest of the trick should be a breeze.

When the spectator is asked to find the letter that corresponds with her number, it will not take her long to discover that the correct letter is D (since D is the fourth letter of the alphabet).

Now the spectator has to think of a country that begins with the letter D. So what are her choices? Let's take a look:

Denmark
Dominican Republic
Dominica
Djibouti

Let's assume that no one on the planet will pick Djibouti (unless, of course, she just returned from a safari on the outskirts of Ethiopia). It is also a safe bet that no one will answer Dominica, since no one has ever heard of this country (including a disturbing portion of the 74,000 people who live on this Caribbean island).

That leaves us with Denmark and the Dominican Republic. And because most people think that the Dominican Republic is a suburb of Mexico, this option can safely be eliminated from consideration. Leaving us with:

Denmark.

On the numerous occasions when I have performed this demonstration, Denmark has been selected *every* time. Rest assured that the trick will not be derailed at this point.

The next step for the spectator in this seemingly never ending series of tasks is to think of an animal that begins with the *last* letter of her selected country (**K** for Denmar**K**). An animal beginning with K. Let's take a look at her options:

First, there's the adorable kori bustard. I'd stake the farm that this short-billed, omnivorous East African crane will not be the first "K" animal to appear in the mind of your spectator. Neither will the king vulture or the Komodo dragon lizard. (Of course, there's the laughing "King of the Bush" kookaburra, who, if truth be known, is far too busy sitting on the old gum tree to have any time to be an unwitting part of a mind-reading escapade—no matter how breathtaking.)

Yes, eliminating those improbable "K" animals, the field has been considerably narrowed:

Kangaroo   and   *Koala*

From the hundreds of different animals on the planet, the field of choices is limited to these two marsupials. And when it comes right down to it, pouched animals tend to be selected at far greater intervals than their non-pouched cousins. If you ask me, I'd count on kangaroo every time. (I will admit, however, that I have been tripped up with "kitten." Don't let this deter you! More often than not the answer will be kangaroo).

Now that the spectator has selected her animal, she must perform one last task before her nightmarish ordeal is over. Taking the last letter of her animal (**O** for kangaro**O**), she is asked to name a fruit. Again, let's examine her choices:

First and foremost there's "orange." Having a hard time coming up with an "O" fruit other than orange? Don't feel bad; you aren't alone. Not many people are familiar with otaheite gooseberries. Are you thinking, "Hey, what about 'ovacado,' dude?" Well, don't. Because in the first place it's "avocado" and in the second, don't call me dude.

I admit that it is possible that someone will say "olive," but hardly anyone knows that this is a fruit. Most people think it's meat.

Let's review.
  Pick a number: 3
  Multiply by 9: 27
  Add digits together: 9
  Subtract 5: 4
  Corresponding letter: D
  Name a country: Denmark
  Name an animal: Kangaroo
  Name a fruit: Orange
  Were you thinking of a **kangaroo** *eating an* **orange** *in* **Denmark**??

Tips & Techniques

As is true for most mind-reading demonstrations, the impact of this trick will depend on how well you can "sell" it to the audience. Remember that most people who see you perform this trick won't be aware of the number nine phenomenon and will think that you are actually able to predict their choices. So it's up to you to play upon the audience's fascination and pretend that you do indeed possess the power to read their thoughts.

Although I generally like to perform these mind-reading tricks as part of a comedy routine, this particular demonstration works best when you play it straight, sprinkled with a touch of humor. Try this:

Ask your volunteer to concentrate and think of a number between 1 and 10. When she signals that she has the number, stop her and say, "You think this is a joke? I asked you

21

to *concentrate* and think of a number; not arbitrarily pick one out of the air. How do you expect me to pick up on your thoughts if you don't try to send me signals?"

After the volunteer says she has concentrated and is thinking of a number, place your hand on her forehead as if you are trying to pick up her thoughts through your fingertips and channel them through your hand, up your arm, through your shoulder, into your neck, and finally to your superpowerful and very large brain. Feel free to tell your audience that this is what is happening as you do it. Tell her that she selected an excellent number and then have her perform the next several steps. Continue this unsettling behavior as she makes her selections.

If you prefer, instead of reading her thoughts, you can pretend to channel them into her head. This, unfortunately, causes you considerable pain—and it shows from your facial expressions. Using this approach, you will ask your subject to relax her mind and accept the thoughts coming to her. This tactic is very effective because it encourages her to think of the first thing that pops into her head, making it more likely that she will make the correct selections.

Some Great Endings

You will need to select an entertaining technique to reveal your predictions to your audience. The easiest and most straightforward method is to simply end the trick by announcing:

Are you thinking of a kangaroo eating an orange in Denmark?

Yes, you will receive the standard reactions: *"How did you do that?"* and *"Get me outa here—this guy's crazy!"* and *"Are there any donuts left?"* But if you want to make a lasting impact, add a little spark to your performance. Here's an idea:

Before beginning the demonstration, write the answer on an index card (A kangaroo eating an orange in Denmark). Or, if you are artistically inclined, draw a picture of a kangaroo eating an orange with an arrow pointing to Denmark on a hand-drawn map of Europe (yes, my geographically challenged friend, Denmark is indeed in Europe). Place this index card in an envelope and seal it. When it's time to perform the trick, hand the envelope to a spectator and ask him to hold it until the demonstration is over.

When your volunteer has made her selections, have her announce them to the audience at the conclusion of the trick. Once everyone has heard her choices, ask the spectator holding the envelope to open it and read your predictions. Then quickly get out your digital camera to capture the priceless looks of bewilderment on the faces of your spectators.

If you prefer, you can have an entire group of people (fewer than 10 is preferred) secretly make their selections at the same time. Say that this demonstration will test which members in the audience have ESP. After they have all made their selections, have someone open the envelope, pull out the index card, and read your predictions. Imagine their reactions when they see that you correctly predicted what each and every one of them selected! And if one or two people have different answers (let's face it, every once in a while a kitten will beat out a kangaroo), you can say that their ESP skills have not been fully developed.

A Spectacular Finish

The methods mentioned above are fine for your average, run-of-the-mill, fall-on-the-floor-gasping mind-reading demonstration. But I have a feeling, my mind-reading chum, that you want something a bit more powerful. Well, I won't disappoint. The ending I am about to describe will shake the very souls of your unsuspecting victims. I devised this ending to add some punch to an already remarkable trick. It's fairly intense, so you may want to hold on to something as you read it. Here goes:

Imagine that your volunteer(s) just announced their selections: *Kangaroo, Denmark, Orange.* You then ask the spectator with the envelope to open it up and read what is inside. Instead of a prediction, the index card reveals a telephone number and a name. Huh? You heard me: A telephone number and a name. For the sake of this explanation, let's say that this name is Rodman Neumann.

You now instruct one of your spectators to call this number and ask to speak with Rodman Neumann. When your confused spectator does what you ask, make sure that the phone is set to "speaker" mode so everyone in the room can hear it.

Are you still with me? At this point in the trick, your volunteer has announced her selections and the audience is gathered around the speakerphone waiting for a brilliant conclusion to all this madness. When the spectator asks to speak to Rodman Neumann, the audience hears, *"I'm sorry, but Rodman went to Denmark to ride a kangaroo and pick oranges."*

Hello? Do you see what just happened here? This "stranger" on the telephone delivered the conclusion in an unfathomable way. Do you own a defibrillator and smelling salts? You may want to invest in them, as you will most likely have to use them to revive your audience. They will, however, need many months of therapy to get over what they witnessed, but it is a small price to pay for you to establish your reputation as the greatest mind reader of all time.

Oh, and who answered the telephone? It's a friend of yours, of course. When your friend hears the cue "Rodman Neumann," he will know to respond. It is important to use a really unusual name so that your friend will automatically know how to respond. Feel free to use Rodman Neumann, as it is highly unlikely that anyone would have such a bizarre name.

4

$\mathcal{P}$ower of $\mathcal{N}$ine, $\mathcal{P}$art 2: $\mathcal{A}$lice in $\mathcal{N}$umberland

DIFFICULTY LEVEL: ✦✦✦✦✦
IMPACT: ✹✹✳✳✳ (WARM-UP)
TECHNIQUE: MATHEMATICS
RISK: ✔✔✔✔✔

Overview

Lewis Carroll, author of *Alice's Adventures in Wonderland,* was also a gifted mathematician who understood the power of the number nine. In addition to writing about nervous white rabbits and smirking Cheshire cats, he was also known to have devised a mathematical trick or two. He is credited with coming up with the following demonstration.

Premise

In this demonstration, the mind reader will accurately predict the total of what appear to be random numbers offered by volunteers and the mind reader.

Step 1: A sheet of paper is placed on a table with the numbers 1 through 5 written down the side. A spectator is asked to write down a four-digit number next to the number 1.

Step 2: When the mind reader sees the number, he writes down his own four-digit number on an index card (making sure the spectators cannot see what he writes). He then folds his index card, seals it in an envelope, and places it on the table. This is the prediction that will be read at the conclusion of the trick.

Step 3: Another spectator is asked to write down a three-digit number next to the number 2 on the paper.

Step 4: The mind reader then writes his own three-digit number next to the number 3 on the paper.

Step 5: Repeat Step 3 and Step 4: A spectator writes down a three-digit number next to the number 4 on the paper, and the mind reader writes a three-digit number next to the number 5.

Step 6: The five numbers on the piece of paper are added together and the total is announced. This number will match the prediction written on the index card in the envelope.

But how? Why? Who? Where? Okay, calm down, have a cup of tea, and read the answer to Lewis Carroll's trick below.

Solution

Once again, it's mathematics and the number nine at work in this clever demonstration. Let's look at each step to see why this works:

After placing a piece of paper on the table (numbered downward 1 through 5), you asked a volunteer to write a four-digit number next to the number 1. For the sake of this explanation, let's assume that the number was **5782**. As mentioned in Step 2, you will write down your prediction on an index card. But how on earth will you know what number to write down? Easy! Follow this formula, and you will be correct every time: Add a 2 to the first number and subtract a 2 from the last number. So, after seeing **5782,** you will write the number **7780** on your index card, and then fold it up and put it on the table.

The next part is just as easy. In Step 3, you asked a spectator to write down a three-digit number. You then have to write a three-digit number directly below his. Let's assume that the number your volunteer wrote was **537.** Here is where our friend the number 9 comes in. Your job is to make sure that *each digit adds up to 9.* What do I mean by that? Since the volunteer's first digit was 5, then your first digit will be 4. Your volunteer wrote **537,** so your number will be **462.**

26

You then repeat this step with another volunteer. If she writes **278,** you will counter with **721.** At this point in the trick, the paper should look as follows:

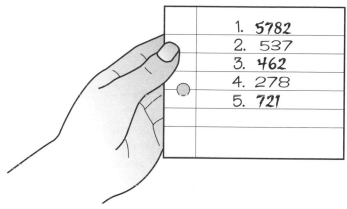

1. *5782*
2. 537
3. *462*
4. 278
5. *721*

Then all you have to do to bring this demonstration to a successful conclusion is have another volunteer add up the numbers. And a quick calculation would give us a total of: (let's see, carry the 2 . . . add the 9 . . .) **7780!**

WHY IT WORKS

Does it matter why it works? Must you know everything? Can't you leave well enough alone?? Okay, if you insist on knowing the *why* behind the *how,* here it is:

Remember the four-digit number that your first volunteer wrote down next to number one (5782)? Well, your job was to add a 2 to the first digit and then subtract 2 from the last digit, making a total of 7780 as your secret prediction. In essence, what you just did was add **1998** to your volunteer's number.

Why is that significant? Take a look:

After your second volunteer wrote down his three-digit number (537), you wrote down 462, making sure the two digits in each column totaled 9. What you really did was guarantee that the total of your number and his number equaled 999 (See? 537 + 462 = 999). You then did it again with the next volunteer (278 + 721 = 999).

And if you add 999 + 999 what do you get? **1998!** Do you see where this is going? By adding the 1998 to the original number 5782, you get the number you wrote on the prediction card: **7780!**

Tips & Techniques

The reason you ask your first volunteer to write down a four-digit number in Step 1 is to throw off your audience. It is more difficult for people to figure out the 1998 "coincidence" if you camouflage it with a four-digit number. You are so tricky.

Here are a few hints to keep in mind:

When you write down your three-digit numbers, it must not appear as if you are calculating. If you take too long, the spectators will accuse you of adding numbers to make sure they match your prediction. If you write your numbers quickly, you will eliminate that suspicion.

The only number you can take your time writing is the prediction number on the index card. Feel free to consult the heavens or even make a telephone call to ask a "psychic advisor" what number you should predict. At this point in the trick, time is not of the essence, and you can use as much of it as you like—as long as it is entertaining!

Have you thought about how you are going to present the dramatic finish to this trick? Remember, when your audience sees that the prediction you made on the index card matches the grand total on the paper, they will be frozen in their seats, stunned at the brilliance of your powers. Use this to your advantage.

But before you shake their world, make sure that you emphasize how remarkable it would be if the numbers match. Point out the randomness of the trick: The three volunteers had complete freedom to choose whatever three- or four-digit numbers they desired—without any influence from you. This will make the ending seem even more incredible.

$\mathcal{A}$cute $\mathcal{S}$enses

DIFFICULTY LEVEL: ✦✦✦✦✦
IMPACT: ✴✴✴✴✴ (WARM-UP)
TECHNIQUES: PARTNER/SIMPLE CODE
RISK: ✔✔✔✔✔

Overview

This amusing demonstration is designed for small groups of people and is great to use in conjunction with other tricks. It allows the mind reader to use showmanship and humor in a dazzling display of mentalism.

Premise

Once the mind reader leaves the room, the group selects a person in the audience. The mind reader then returns to the room and identifies the person who was selected.

Solution

For the sake of this explanation, let's assume that there are six people in the audience. In a casual social setting, most groups will be seated in a circle or square in a portion of the room.

After the person in the group has been selected, your partner will call you back into the room. *The words that the partner uses will indicate which person was selected.* Working clockwise, if the person chosen is sitting directly next to your partner, only one word will be used to call you into the room. If the selected person is sitting two people from your partner (clockwise), two words will be used; three people over will equal three words, and so on. Here are some suggestions that you can use for up to six people:

One: Ready!

Two: Come in!

Three: Come in now!

Four: We're ready for you!

Five: You can come in now!

Six: We are ready for you now!

See how easy that is? It can work over and over as long as your partner is the one calling you into the room each time.

Tips & Techniques

When you return to the room, you will be able to quickly figure out who the secret person is by using the above method. But instead of pointing out the person right away, pretend that you need to perform a psychic exercise to determine who was selected.

Announce that the reason that you are able to read minds and perform psychic feats is that you have heightened senses. Say that the person who was selected is hiding a secret, and when someone has a secret, that makes him emit a slight odor. In order to identify the secret person, you will have to use your sense of smell.

Am I suggesting that you walk around the room sniffing the people? You bet I am! (Oh, is sniffing people too low-class for you? Well, *excuuuuuse* me. In my day, sniffing people was a sign of respect.) Believe me, it is wildly entertaining. Imagine their reactions as you walk from person to person, inhaling deeply from various parts of their bodies. You sniff deeply and then concentrate as you try to determine who was selected. When you reach the person who was chosen, make it seem as if you aren't sure. Another deep sniff of a different part of his body clears up all suspicions.

Not comfortable with the idea of smelling everyone in the room? Okay, no problem. Everyone has his or her hang-ups. Here is another suggestion: Instead of your sense of smell, use your sense of touch. Walk around the room feeling everyone's head, exclaiming that you can actually get vibrations from each person's brain and determine who was selected.

Still not your cup of tea? I understand. Then try your sense of hearing. Have each person in the room sing the chorus of "Three Blind Mice" or the theme to *Gilligan's Island* or another equally absurd song. Then, judging by their tonal quality, you can determine the person who was selected.

Variations

If you are performing the demonstration for friends and you know their voices, you can involve the audience in giving you the clues. In this instance, your partner will ask someone in the group to call you back into the room. When you return, you will be able to identify the person selected immediately. How? It's easy! Whoever called you into the room will be sitting *directly next to* (clockwise) the person who was selected. Or, to make it a little less obvious, the person who calls you back into the room will be sitting *two seats* (clockwise) from the person who was selected.

Another method that can be used is to look at the position of your partner's right arm. It will be pointing in the direction of the person selected. Or, for five people or less, your partner can casually leave his hand on the table with his fingers indicating how many people over (clockwise) the secret person is. If you repeat the demonstration, you can alternate these techniques to keep the audience guessing.

Obviously, if there are too many people in the room, the trick becomes unwieldy and impractical. Can you imagine performing this trick at a party with fifty guests, and from the next room you hear your partner say, "Okay—you—can—come—in—now—we—are—ready—for—you—to—come—back—in—and—tell—us—who—the—secret—person—is . . . now." So it may be best to save this trick for smaller gatherings.

When performed properly, this quick, clever technique can set the stage for one of the more spectacular demonstrations described in this book. For example, some tricks require a volunteer to be selected from the audience. You can use this method to figure out which audience member volunteered for the trick. By itself or with another trick, this will add a fun demonstration to your repertoire.

31

X-Ray Mentalism

6

DIFFICULTY LEVEL: ✦✦✦✦✦
IMPACT: ✵✵✵✵✵ (✵✵✵✵✵ ON SECOND VERSION)
TECHNIQUE: SWITCHING
RISK: ✔✔✔✔✔

Overview

I invented this trick to create the illusion that my mental powers are so strong, they can pierce through a thick barrier. Just as a weight lifter proves his physical strength by ripping a phone book in half, I prove my psychic ability by naming a card that was placed deep inside a thick phone book.

Premise

The mentalist instructs a spectator to shuffle a deck thoroughly. When the audience is satisfied that the cards are random, the mind reader asks the host of the party if he can borrow a telephone book. Once the book is produced, the mind reader asks another spectator to select a card, and—without looking at it—place it deep inside of the telephone book, facedown.

The mind reader then announces that he will attempt to "read" the card, despite the fact that it is buried hundreds of pages within the recesses of this very thick book. After intense concentration and some psychic muscle flexing, he then writes his answer on a slip of paper and seals it inside an envelope. This envelope is given to another spectator for safekeeping.

The mind reader then opens the phone book, retrieves a card, and places it facedown on the table. The spectator with the envelope is asked to open it and reveal the prediction. With much suspense, the mind reader asks another spectator to flip over the card and see whether it matches the prediction. Was there ever a doubt? Once again, the mind reader has proven his superior mental ability.

Solution

Can you imagine the bewildered look on your audience's faces when they see you accurately name a card that was randomly selected and placed deep inside a telephone book?

How is this done? Voodoo? Witchcraft? *Magic?* Hardly. In fact, the solution could not be any simpler. How will you know the identity of the card inside the telephone book? Because you put it there. Yes, I kid you not. *You put it there.* Before you begin the trick, you have to sneak a card into the telephone book at your friend's house. And it should go without saying that you must memorize this card because it will be the card that you are going to write as your prediction later.

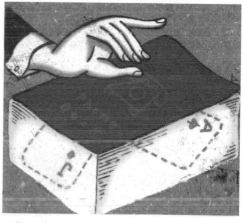

I know what you're thinking: *But how? When? Why? Where will I find his phone book? Did I leave the oven on? Was it ethical to replace the original Darren on Bewitched with Dick Sargent in 1969?* Easy does it, my curious mind-reading friend. Would I ever ask you to do something that I haven't already done successfully numerous times? Have faith! I will show you several easy methods in Tips & Techniques.

At the beginning of the trick, you asked a spectator to slide a card into the telephone book, facedown. Remember, you instructed him *not* to look at the card. In fact, no one in the room was able to see the card. So when you pull the card from the telephone book to conclude the demonstration, your audience will assume that this is the card that the spectator placed in it a few moments ago. And why wouldn't they? I mean, you'd never do something as devious as planting a second card . . . *or would you?*

33

So before you make a prediction, there will be two cards in the telephone book. Obviously, the card you write down as your prediction will be the one you sneaked in the phone book earlier. As long as you pull out the correct card, the trick will work flawlessly.

Worried? Nervous? Don't be. Help is on the way!

Tips & Techniques

Let's first address your greatest concern. How are you going to get your hands on your friend's telephone book? Here are some options:

If you are performing this trick in your house or that of a close friend, you may already know where the telephone book is. If you plan to perform this trick in the future, find out where he keeps his phone book on an earlier visit. In many cases, however, the book will be easily accessible.

If you are unable to secure a telephone book, then you can use any other book in the house. If you're in his kitchen, you can probably find a recipe book; if you're in his living room, there's most likely a coffee table book around; if you're in his bedroom . . . well, then I'd have to wonder what you're doing in your friend's bedroom in the first place. Wherever you are, select any book that is handy (the bigger the better) and firmly implant a card inside.

This is a great demonstration to perform in an office. Telephone books are almost always out in the open. I've gotten so used to performing this trick that whenever I am in someone's office, I automatically sneak a card into the telephone book. This way I am always prepared to perform this feat at a moment's notice—even if it's weeks later.

It is a great effect when the audience sees you asking the host to borrow his phone book. This practically eliminates any suspicion that you tampered with it beforehand. It will seem so natural that no one will even consider the possibility that you hid a card in the book.

Since there will be two cards in the telephone book, it is important that you pull out the correct one. This will be easy if you memorize where you put it. Memorizing the exact page number will be quite helpful. If you have to

34

sneak it in quickly, a general idea of its location should work fine, but it could cause a problem if the spectator inserts his card too close to yours. The best place to put the card is as close to the middle as possible. When inserting it, secure it snugly by the binding so that it will not slip out when the spectator places his card inside.

When looking through the book for the card, you must appear as if you are casually scanning the pages rather than hunting down a specific page. After practicing this several times, you will get the hang of it.

Another crucial part of this trick occurs when you ask a spectator to place the card in the telephone book. Ideally, you want him to put the card somewhere in the middle of the book. This way, it will be believable that you are searching in that general area when you retrieve the card. The best way to get the spectator to place the card toward the middle is to ask him to bury the card directly in the heart of the phone book. Tell him that you want the card as insulated as possible. This usually gets the spectator aiming for the middle of the book.

HAVING SOME FUN
This trick gives you a great opportunity to show the audience that there is a fine line between being a psychic and being a psycho. Let your spectators see the bizarre rituals you have to perform to engage your mental powers. After the spectator places the card in the phone book, be as creative as you like in trying to figure out what it is. Here are a few suggestions:

As in Chapter 5, "Acute Senses," you can use your sense of smell to make your prediction. Claim that each card in the deck gives off its own unique smell, and that you can sense what it is, even buried in hundreds of pages.

Sweet-talk the phone book. Flatter it; kiss it; hug it. Try talking nicely to the phone book to get it to reveal the identity of the card it is holding.

Take out a calculator and perform complex equations, as if the answer has a mathematical basis. After several minutes of fierce calculations, scribble your answer on a piece of paper and slide it in the envelope.

There is one last detail that you should tend to before you can consider your job over. When the demonstration has ended, find an opportunity to remove the second card from the telephone book. If the trick is done properly, your audience should never consider the telephone book a possibility for deception. This is especially true since you asked to borrow it from your host. Still, if you have a chance to get rid of the second card without getting caught, do so.

A Breathtaking Version

There is something that you can do to turn this dazzling feat into a remarkable mind-reading demonstration that will cement your reputation as a premier psychic. But I warn you, it requires some additional planning. Similar to the ending I suggested in Chapter 3, "Power of Nine," you can create a lasting impression by applying some extra effort.

In this version, you do not make a prediction. Instead, you will tell the audience about a friend of yours. You say that although you possess highly advanced mind-reading skills, you are a mere novice compared to your friend, the Exalted Mystic Supreme. In fact, his talents are so powerful that he can identify what card has been placed in the phone book from *thousands of miles away.* And this can be accomplished through the miracle that we call the telephone.

After the spectator places the card in the telephone book, you instruct him to call your friend. Write down the telephone number and have the spectator ask politely for the Exalted Mystic Supreme.

Stress the importance of being polite to the Mystic Supreme, or else he will not be willing to help. Suggest that the spectator practice being polite before he makes the call. Role-play the conversation with him, giving him advice and stopping him when he isn't being polite enough. *"No, no. Flatter him more. Tell him how pretty his donkey is. Compliment his eye patch."*

When you think that your spectator is being sufficiently polite, give him the go-ahead to make the call. Obviously, you will have alerted a friend of yours to expect a telephone call around a certain time that evening. And when someone calls and asks for the Exalted Mystic Supreme, he is to tell them that the card is a jack of clubs (or whatever card you had preselected).

If your friend is a bit of a ham, he could have fun with the spectator by testing his politeness or asking irrelevant questions or even having him perform embarrassing tasks for the psychic powers to take effect.

When the Exalted Mystic Supreme finally does reveal the card (via speakerphone), it is time to present the grand finale. As in the original version, you locate the card, place it facedown on the table, and ask a spectator to turn it over. Then stand back and smile as you watch your befuddled audience desperately try to come up with the solution.

If you don't mind enlisting the help of a partner, you will find that this version will have audiences mystified for months to come.

7

A Dollar for Your Thoughts

DIFFICULTY LEVEL: ✦✦✦✦✦ (HIGHER IN THE ADVANCED VERSION)
IMPACT: ✳✳✳✳✳
TECHNIQUE: SWITCHING
RISK: ✔✔✔✔✔

Overview

This trick uses an easy sleight of hand technique that I first discussed in one of my earlier books *Mystifying Mind Reading Tricks.* The method is easy to master and the effect is so stunning that it's worth another look in a different demonstration. A double switch variation is presented at the end that is less easy.

Premise

The mind reader hands a spectator an index card and a pencil and asks her to write down a three-digit number. Once this is done, the mind reader takes the index card and hands it to another spectator, asking that he, too, write a three-digit number on the same card—directly below the first number.

And, finally, the mind reader asks a third spectator to write a three-digit number below the other two numbers. So now there are three three-digit numbers on an index card, one below another.

The mind reader then asks for a volunteer to add up the three three-digit numbers. The sum of these numbers will produce a four-digit number. When the volunteer reaches a total, he is asked to announce it to the audience. And then . . .

The mind reader thinks about the four-digit number that was just announced. After a moment, he exclaims that this number sounds very familiar to him. Finally it dawns upon him where he saw this number before. From his pocket, the mind reader produces a one-dollar bill and gives it to a spectator. He then asks the spectator to read off the first four digits in the serial number. Lo and behold—a perfect match!

Solution

As you can well imagine, audiences do not recover quickly from a psychic demonstration such as this. I mean—the dollar . . . the numbers . . . the coincidence . . . *how??* Your audience had free will to write down any three-digit numbers they chose. Then how on earth is it possible that the sum of three freely chosen numbers matches the first four digits on the dollar bill? The only plausible explanation is that you psychically penetrated the minds of the spectators and mentally forced them to write down the numbers you wanted.

Actually the solution is a lot less dramatic. Before you begin the trick, you will select a one-dollar bill and note the first four digits. You then write down three three-digit numbers on an index card—one under another as described above. You must make sure that the total of these three numbers equals the first four digits on the dollar bill. Then the stage is set for your performance.

Here's the solution: The index card that the participants used to write down their numbers *will not* be the one that you hand to the final spectator to be totaled. Instead, you will switch their index card with the one that you secretly prepared ahead of time. But how will you make the switch? Let's take a closer look at the demonstration to see how this can be accomplished.

When you begin the demonstration, you will be holding a small stack of four or five index cards in your hand. The bottom index card will be the one you prepared before the trick. Remember, after the spectators have written their numbers, they will hand you back the index card. Place it on top of your stack. *So now you have the spectators' card on top of your stack and your phony card on the bottom.*

You then ask for a volunteer to add the numbers. When you select someone, the audience is usually distracted momentarily as they look at the volunteer. This would be a great time to flip the index cards over. *So now the top card is your phony card.* The audience's card is now on the bottom.

And, since you planned it ahead of time, you know that the total of the numbers will indeed match the first four digits on the dollar bill in the envelope. All that's left to do is have the numbers announced and call 9-1-1 to revive the audience.

Tips & Techniques

The index card switch is quick and relatively low-risk. Since the audience has no idea what you are planning with the index cards, no one will suspect that you're trying to make a switch. All you have to do is *turn over* your stack of index cards. There are many ways to do this without being detected. I usually raise my stack of cards in the air and ask for a volunteer to add the numbers. When I bring my arm down, I transfer the cards from my left hand to my right, casually turning the stack over. Then I hand the top card to the final spectator to be totaled.

Caution: When placing the two index cards on your stack, *make sure that the writing faces in.* This way, no one will be able to see that the top and bottom cards have handwriting on them.

When you are preparing your phony index card before the demonstration, you must write each entry in different handwriting. If you don't, it won't take long for the final spectator to notice that all three numbers were written exactly the same.

Let's talk about the dollar bill. You will have to find a one-dollar bill where the first four digits start with a 1 or a 2. This is because the most that the total of the three three-digit numbers can possibly be is 2,997—assuming each spectator wrote down 999. Preferably, the first four digits will range between 1000 and 2000. This way you can set up your index cards without having to use all high numbers—which may be noted or questioned by the final spectator.

The mind-reading aspect of this demonstration comes into play when the spectators are writing their three-digit numbers. When the participants are about to write their numbers, you have to "transmit" your thoughts to them, attempting to influence their decision. To meet this end you may want to try placing your hand on their foreheads or chanting to them in a made-up language. You can tell them that if they concentrate on their numbers, something spectacular usually ensues.

The best part of this exhibition is the conclusion. After your final spectator announces the four-digit total, you pretend that the number sounds familiar, but you are not sure why. Take a moment to act confused and ask the audience whether anyone present recognizes the number. Suddenly, you have a suspicion of where you have seen that number before. Retrieve your wallet from your pocket, open it, and pull out a dollar bill (or perhaps a hundred-dollar bill, Mr. Moneybags?). Act startled as you study the bill. Then hand it to a spectator and ask him to read the first four digits of the serial number. Then take your bows, revel in the applause, and try to remember to get your money back!

The Double Switch Variation

I hate to even mention this version to you because it is fraught with extra risk and requires greater effort. This variation does not fall into the "easy" category, but I feel that I would be negligent if I didn't at least mention how you can make this demonstration even more amazing (is that even possible?).

41

At the beginning of the demonstration, ask someone to hand you a dollar bill. When an audience member offers a dollar, say, "Thank you; tips are appreciated."

In this version, you have two options. The first is to keep the dollar in your hand for the duration of the trick. At some point, however, you will have to switch it with the dollar bill that you had already preselected for this demonstration. There will be plenty of opportunity for you to do this if you have the bill concealed in the palm of one of your hands. If you want an easier switch, then put the bill in your shirt pocket. When it is time to present the conclusion, reach into that same pocket and produce the preselected bill instead.

Your second option is a lot riskier. You have to make a quick switch of the dollar bill and then give it to a spectator to hold for safekeeping until the end of the trick. This is, by far, a more effective ending, but requires you to execute a rather tricky maneuver. Once you get a dollar bill from a spectator, fold it in half and in half again as you ask for a volunteer to hold the bill. Now that the bill is folded twice, it is small enough for you to make a quick switch and hand the volunteer your preselected dollar.

When the four-digit number is announced, conclude the demonstration by asking the volunteer with the dollar bill to read aloud the first four digits of the serial number.

Whichever version you decide to use, A Dollar for Your Thoughts is one of several showstoppers that are described in this book. It is a perfect demonstration to conclude your routine and leave your audience with a lasting impression.

*P*erfect *P*rediction

8

DIFFICULTY LEVEL: ✦✦✦✦✦
IMPACT: ✳✳✳✳✳
TECHNIQUE: PRESET PREDICTIONS
RISK: ✔✔✔✔✔

Overview

One of the primary job responsibilities of a psychic is to be able to predict events before they occur. It says so right in the job description. So, to make sure you are up to speed on the basic expectations of a mind reader, I'd like to teach you a simple trick you can use to predict a future event. (After all, I'd hate to see you get fired!)

Premise

The mind reader places three objects on a table: a key, an envelope, and a coin. He then announces that he will attempt to transmit his thoughts telepathically to a member of the audience. A volunteer is chosen and asked to select one of the objects. Once the spectator has announced her selection, the mind reader shows the audience that he knew what she was going to pick all along.

Solution

It couldn't be easier! All you have to do is guess which object was chosen by the spectator. Easier said than done, you say? Well, if it really was purely a guess then you would have a 33 percent chance of getting it right. But 33 percent is hardly a guarantee that you will pull this trick off successfully, now, is it? Wouldn't it be great if you could improve those chances, to more like 100 percent? Well, that might make a nervous mind reader feel more relaxed. There's nothing I like more than a trick that is practically foolproof. And that's what we have here.

Whichever object is selected, you will be able to show the audience that you predicted it ahead of time. You will prove this by showing that you wrote your prediction down before the demonstration began. Here's how:

Let's assume that your spectator chose the envelope. Once she announces her selection, you simply turn over the envelope. Written on the back of the envelope is the phrase *I knew you'd pick the envelope!*

But, you are sure to ask, what if she doesn't pick the envelope? Excellent question! After all, statistically, the spectator will choose the envelope only one out of every three times. Not to worry; I have a way out.

If the spectator selects the coin, you pick up the envelope, open it, and remove a smaller envelope from inside. Flip it over to reveal the phrase *I knew you'd pick the coin!*

And finally, if the key is selected, you open the second envelope to reveal an index card. Written on the index card is the phrase *I knew you'd pick the key!*

Do you see how this works? Because you apparently made your prediction before the trick began, it will appear as if you *really knew* what the spectator would choose.

Tips & Techniques

Although this trick works well no matter what object is chosen, it is much more dramatic if the spectator selects the key (the one you predicted on the index card). It will appear as if you are toying with the audience by hiding the answer in an envelope inside another envelope. Take your time removing the envelope, explaining that you used extra precautions to hide your prediction. You trained with the FBI to learn the top secret "index-card-inside-an-envelope-inside-yet-another-envelope" technique for protecting highly confidential information. I mean, it's one thing for you to steal someone's thoughts, but you certainly don't want your stolen thoughts stolen. Caution: If the key is selected, remember to keep the backs of both envelopes hidden from the audience.

The first thing you will want to do upon completion of the trick is to pack up your props. Once you identify the mystery object, you have to move quickly to hide or destroy the incriminating evidence. Let's face it—if someone decides to examine your envelopes, you will be exposed as the cheating fraud that you are and run out of town. To avoid this embarrassing and potentially life-threatening situation, casually clear away your props as you divert the audience's attention by talking up your next demonstration.

As you may have figured out by now, you can perform this demonstration only one time in front of each audience. How long do you think it would take for your observers to catch on to the fact that you have three different predictions already prepared? Once you finish this trick, move on to another one. *Do not repeat this trick for the same audience—no matter how much they beg!*

Poker Party

DIFFICULTY LEVEL: ✦✦✦✦✦
IMPACT: ✷✷✷✷✷ (WARM-UP)
TECHNIQUE: MATHEMATICS
RISK: ✔✔✔✔✔

Overview

It's such a pleasure to perform a trick where there is no preparation, nor any complicated maneuvers to perform, and no partners to get in your way. In Poker Party, we let mathematics do all the dirty work for us. As long as you follow some very easy steps, this trick will work flawlessly every time.

Poker Party is a great trick to perform for a small group of people. And if you play poker, this is a perfect demonstration for when it's your turn to deal.

Premise

Step 1: The mind reader deals poker hands (five cards each) to five players.

Step 2: Each player is asked to shuffle his or her cards and select one mentally.

Step 3: The mind reader gathers the cards from each player (keeping them in the same order) and then deals five rows of five cards—each face up on the table.

Step 4: Each player is asked which row contains his or her card. Even though there are five cards in the row, the mind reader is able to correctly name each person's card.

46

Solution

The answer to this easy and effective demonstration lies in the way you gather and deal the cards. Let's look at this trick in more detail:

The first step is straightforward. You deal five poker hands (five cards each) to five players. After they each shuffle their cards and mentally select one, you gather the cards from them. But! You cannot simply grab all the cards and clump them into a pile. You must collect the cards in order. Starting from your left, take the first player's cards and then work your way around the table until everyone's cards have been collected.

Each time you take a player's cards, stack them underneath the cards you have already collected. By doing this, you guarantee that the first player's cards are on the top of your pile, and the last player's cards are on the bottom of the pile.

Does this make sense? Are you with me so far?

Then all you have to do is deal five rows of five cards on the table. But it is important that you deal the cards *going from left to right.*

Once you have dealt the first row of cards, continue making rows until all of the cards have been dealt. When you are done, you will have five rows of five cards each.

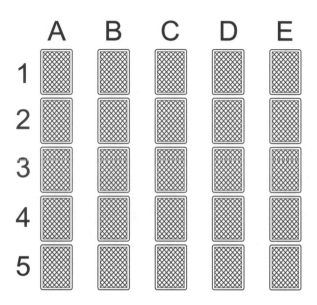

Can you see what has happened here? You just laid out the five players' poker hands in five neat little rows:

Player 1's poker hand = Row #1

Player 2's poker hand = Row #2

Player 3's poker hand = Row #3

Player 4's poker hand = Row #4

Player 5's poker hand = Row #5

So! Knowing this, all you have to do is ask each player to point to the column (A through E) that contains his or her card. It will be crystal clear which cards were selected since *each player only has one card in each vertical column*. To make a lasting impression, present their cards in an entertaining finish.

Tips & Techniques

The best feature of *Poker Party* is that mathematics does all the dirty work. All you have to do is gather and deal the cards correctly, and you can't go wrong. The only snag to this trick is that it's quite possible that there will be at least one wise guy in your audience who will figure out the solution. Not to worry! Here is how you can throw off the troublemakers.

You are at your most vulnerable to get caught when you are dealing the cards into rows on the table. Your job is to distract them so that they do not notice that the hands they were originally dealt are being laid out on the table in neat little rows. As you are dealing, divert the audience's attention by explaining the psychic quality of cards. You can say, "Did you know that the use of playing cards can be found as far back as the thirteenth century?" (Which, by the way, is entirely true.) "And not only did people in medieval times use playing cards for gambling and games of skill, they also used them to tell fortunes." (Which is also true!) By the time you finish with your history lesson, the cards will be dealt and you can proceed with the conclusion of the trick.

Presenting the Conclusion

One tip to keep in mind: When revealing the secret cards, do not ask the spectators in order. This way the audience will be less likely to notice that the rows are lined up in the same order as the spectators.

Once the cards have been laid out on the table in five rows of five cards each, take a moment to survey the arrangement and prepare yourself for a crucial mind-reading exercise. Ask the spectators for total silence while you summon your psychic powers. When the mood has been set, randomly choose a spectator and ask him which row (A through E) contains his secret card. Your audience will see you concentrating intensely, eyes closed, as your hand moves over each card. After a few seconds, the aura from one of the cards is so strong that it causes you to gasp and freeze your position. Your breathing becomes labored as your trembling hand slowly reaches down and touches the secret card.

49

You pick it up and show it to him. There's no need to ask whether this card is his; *you know it is.* Let the audience ask the spectator whether you were correct.

Place the card aside on the table and select another spectator. Again, ask which row her card is in. Once she tells you the row, you instantly know her card—but don't merely blurt it out! This time, when you feel the aura of the cards, do not stop on the one that she picked. Instead, pick one up and toss it off the table. Then pick another one from the same row and discard it as well. Soon, four of the five cards will be gone, leaving only the secret card that she chose. Pick it up, hold it out to show the audience, and put it with the first spectator's card. Remember, there is no reason to verify that this card is correct—*you know it is.*

Each time you reveal another spectator's card, try to do it a little differently—especially if you know personal information about your audience. For example, let's say that one of the cards chosen is a seven of hearts. Instead of "psychically" naming the card, you can say that it wasn't even necessary this time, since you knew that this spectator's birthday is on the seventh. In most cases—if you use your imagination—you will be able to make a connection between the selected card and the spectator. Even if the connection is vague and far-fetched, you will still get the card correct, so it won't matter.

Perhaps you need to perform a bizarre scientific experiment on the cards to figure out which one was selected. One way of doing this is to pour droplets of water on each card, swirl the water around, and then watch closely as the water runs off the card. Then you can scribble down notes furiously as if you are recording data from the experiment. Continue to do this to each card in the row. When you are finished, examine your notes and hold up the correct card—as if the water droplets had something to do with it.

Poker Party provides you the opportunity to be as creative as you like in the presentation. Make yourself stand out from other performers by adding your own imaginative twists to the trick. Let them ridicule your methods all they want. When they see that you've gotten every card correct, you'll be the one left laughing as they will be forced to acknowledge your superior mental talents.

*W*rite *O*n

DIFFICULTY LEVEL: ◆◆◆◆◆
IMPACT: ✳✳✳✳✳ (WARM-UP)
TECHNIQUES: SECRET CODE/UNMITIGATED GALL/
                 FAITH IN THE HUMAN RACE
RISK: ✔✔✔✔✔

Overview

Write On is a great warm-up trick to get the audience in the right spirit for mind reading. What's different about this trick is that the mind reader is at the complete mercy of a spectator. I always find myself holding my breath hoping that my volunteer catches on quickly.

Premise

The mind reader explains to her audience that everyone is born with the power to transmit and interpret thoughts. It's merely a matter of harnessing this power through practice and concentration. To prove this, the mind reader selects an eager volunteer and asks him to step out of the room momentarily.

While he is gone, the mind reader asks the audience to select a number between 1 and 100. Once this has been decided and everyone knows the number, the volunteer is called back into the room. Without any prior planning, this untrained "assistant" is able to name the correct number.

Hey! Wipe that doubting look off your face. Here's how it's done . . .

Solution

The most important part of this trick is to select a volunteer who you think will be able to quickly figure out a simple code. The challenge is that *you never discuss this code with him!*

For the sake of this explanation, let's assume that the audience selected the number **35.** When you call the volunteer back in, make sure that he stands in front of the room facing the audience. You stand next to the spectator and help him concentrate, placing your hand lightly on his back. When there is complete silence in the room and the spectator is concentrating intensely, you *write the number on his back with your finger.* That's right! Simply trace the number 35 on his back.

So you think that I am a few cards short of a full deck for even suggesting that you attempt this? Try it! If done correctly, this trick works most of the time and leaves audiences completely dumbfounded.

Tips & Techniques

To ensure success, you must use careful judgment in selecting a volunteer who you think will:

A. Figure out your code without you telling him;

B. Not blurt out the secret once he feels your creepy fingers crawling on his back; and

C. Act naturally and play along.

It is more effective, however, if the audience decides who the volunteer will be. If they select your assistant, they will be 100 percent sure that he is not a conspirator.

At the beginning of the demonstration, your volunteer will naturally insist that he has absolutely no ability to read minds. Tell him not to worry, explaining that if he concentrates, you will be able to transmit the numbers to him telepathically.

Here are some things you can do to make sure that everything goes smoothly.

Write small on your volunteer's back. People have a tendency to trace large numbers, thinking they are easier to interpret; they're not. If you attempt to write huge, sweeping numbers, it will be more confusing for the volunteer, and your audience will be more likely to see what you are doing. Write small so that just your fingers move and not your entire hand.

Keep talking while you trace the numbers. Pretend that you are trying to concentrate and transmit the numbers. While you are giving verbal encouragement to your volunteer, you will also be distracting the audience members.

Trace the numbers over and over. Write slowly and deliberately. If your volunteer doesn't pick up on your clue right away, keep trying—it will eventually sink in.

When this trick works, it has a powerful impact. After all, it was an audience member who was able to guess the number—not the sneaky, unscrupulous, can't-be-trusted-for-anything mind reader. As long as your volunteer plays along and pretends that the number just "popped into his brain," you will keep the audience scratching their heads for days to come.

As a variation, you can use names instead of numbers. While your volunteer is out of the room, instruct the audience to select the name of someone present. When the volunteer returns, trace that person's name on his back. You should be well practiced in this technique before attempting this version, as it is considerably more challenging.

In a small group, I like to perform this trick several times, using different volunteers. This way, one by one each audience member will get to be included in the trick—until finally only one person remains who doesn't know how it's done. When I finally select this last person as my volunteer, *I don't draw on his back!* It's fun to watch him try hard to figure out the secret number. After all, everyone else was able to do it; why can't he?

Are you thinking that this is far too mean to do to your friends and family? Get over it. Mind reading is a mean and nasty business . . . but so much fun!

53

The Aura of Chalk

DIFFICULTY LEVEL: ✦✦✦✦✦
IMPACT: ✳✳✳✳✳
TECHNIQUE: SLEIGHT OF HAND
RISK: ✔✔✔✔✔

Overview

When you see the devastation that this trick wreaks upon the minds of onlookers, you will understand why the use of chalk and a blindfold in the same trick is outlawed in thirty-seven states and parts of Guam. When you say the name of this demonstration, it is important to use a sweeping hand motion and insert a substantial pause, thus: The Aura . . . of Chalk.

Premise

The mind reader stands in front of the room holding a small blackboard. These blackboards can be found at most discount stores in the school supply section (they're pretty cheap, too). For this experiment, the mind reader asks for four volunteers. The only requirement is that the mind reader must be unfamiliar with the birthdays of the volunteers. The mind reader then asks for someone in the audience to blindfold him. Once the observers are satisfied that he cannot see through the blindfold, the demonstration can begin.

The blindfolded mind reader holds up a blackboard with the numbers 1 through 4 written vertically down the left side. He asks a spectator to write her birthday *next to any one of the numbers* (just the month and day, not the year). When she has accomplished this, the mind reader asks for the blackboard and then proceeds to "feel the aura" over what she has written.

He then asks another spectator to take the blackboard and write down his birthday *next to any available number*. And, once again, the mind reader takes back the blackboard and feels the energy emitted by the chalk. Still blindfolded, the mentalist asks two other spectators to write down their birthdays next to the two available numbers. When this has been accomplished, the mind reader removes his blindfold, studies the dates, and announces which birthday belongs to each spectator.

Solution

When the first spectator hands you the blackboard, hold it in your hands with the writing facing you. While you are waving your hand over the writing, take your index finger and *secretly wipe it down the front of the chalkboard,* leaving a streak in the first birthday. You then hand the chalkboard to the next spectator.

After he has written his birthday next to one of the numbers, he hands you the blackboard. And once again, you secretly run your finger down the slate, creating another streak in the writing. You then repeat this process for the next spectator, creating a third streak in the blackboard.

Finally, you ask the fourth and last spectator to write his birthday next to the only available number. When he hands you back the blackboard you *do not* create another streak with your finger. You will see why in a moment.

At this point in the demonstration, you remove your blindfold and announce that you are about to match the birthdays with the correct participants. As long as you can remember in which order you asked the spectators to write their birthdays, you will have no problem solving the birthday dilemma. And here's how:

the birthday that was written first has three streaks in it;

the birthday that was written second has two streaks in it;

the birthday that was written third has only one streak in it; and

the birthday that was written fourth has *no* streaks in it.

Tips & Techniques

 When you see a date has three streaks in it, you will know that it belongs to the first person you called upon. *So make sure you remember the order in which you called upon your four spectators!* When conducting the demonstration, you decide the order. The easiest way to accomplish this is to have the spectators sit next to each other in a row, and call on them in that order, from left to right. The blackboard is numbered one through four, but you will state that the participants do not have to write their birthdays down in order—they can choose any number that's still available.

Ideally, the streaks you create in the writing will be slight—substantial enough for you to see them, but not so obvious that they would raise the suspicions of the audience. After a few practice runs, you will be able to do this flawlessly. Make your first streak toward the left side of the blackboard, the second streak toward the middle, and the third streak toward the right side. This way, you won't be confused by the streaks crossing paths. Also, instruct your participants to write out the months instead of using abbreviations. This will give you more space to create your streaks.

Another point to consider is the type of blackboard you use. When you are blindfolded, you will have a difficult time discerning which side is the front if both sides are exactly the same—unless you are truly a mind reader (oh, please!). It would be better if you used a blackboard that had the writing

56

side on one side only. This way you will be able to easily tell the front from the back. But if you use a reversible chalkboard, make sure that you attach a small piece of Scotch tape to the front so you will be able to tell by feel which side is the front.

As always, feel free to use any crackpot methods you can devise to activate your mind-reading talents. In The Aura of Chalk, I like to talk about the aura that the chalk emits (hence, the title). I tell my audience:

"Ever since chalk was first discovered in the chalk mines deep in the heart of Angola in the late 1700s, mystics have known about the psychic quality of chalk. It is a well-known fact among psychos—I mean psychics—that when a person touches chalk, a little bit of their essence rubs off on it. And if this essence is interpreted by a properly trained medium (which, of course, I am), then a connection can be made between the *chalk toucher* (a term used by mentalists) and the *touched* (a term used by psychiatrists)."

After bedazzling them with psychic-babble, I proceed to wave my hand mystically around the blackboard, telepathically picking up the vibes that are being transmitted via the chalk crumbs (another psychic term—feel free to use it liberally). I do this each time a participant writes his or her birthday and hands me the blackboard. As you know, this is just a cover to give me an opportunity to run my finger down the blackboard.

Another Version: Telltale Signs

If you have a knowledge of astrology (or have a few minutes to memorize the signs of the zodiac), then you can transform this stunt from a pure mind-reading demonstration into an interesting astrological experiment. After all, psychics and astrologers are all part of the metaphysics family.

State that astrology is an exact science, and that the position of the planets at the time of one's birth determines a person's character, disposition, talents, and weaknesses. To prove that this is true, you would like to conduct an experiment that will demonstrate— once and for all—that the signs of the zodiac are valid and accurate.

You then conduct the demonstration in the same manner as described above. But when it comes time to match the birthdays with the participants, you add an astrological twist:

"I see that one of the birthdays is November twenty-sixth. That's Sagittarius. And, as we all know, Sagittarians are energetic, honest, generous, and fiercely independent. However, they can also be quite pushy, conceited, and vulgar. And if you think about it, those qualities describe Bill perfectly."

Of course, you don't have to be as mean as I am, but let's face facts: A good mind-reading experiment sometimes leaves innocent victims in its wake. And I must admit that, yes, the demonstration works just as well if you're nice to your audience (but it's not as much fun!).

There's no need to memorize the traits for each sign—you can make them up! "This birthday falls under Aquarius. And as we all know, Aquarians are known for their poor fashion sense and appalling taste in music. This must be Ida's birthday."

What if two or more people have the same sign? Well, be creative! "I see two Taurus birthdays, but the May twentieth date is right on the cusp, so there is more of an influence in Gemini. And when we combine the stubbornness of Taurus with the limited intelligence of Gemini, we're led directly to Nick."

If your audience still doubts the validity of astrology, point out that the odds of you correctly matching all four birthdays to all four participants are 23 to 1. That may have them looking at the universe a little differently!

12

*P*age, *L*ine, *W*ord

DIFFICULTY LEVEL: ✦✦✦✦✦
IMPACT: ✹✹✹✹✹ (YUMMY!)
TECHNIQUE: SWITCHING
RISK: ✔✔✔✔✔

Overview

No mind-reading repertoire would be complete without one really good "book test." In Page, Line, Word, you will use your mental powers to predict a word that a spectator randomly picks out of a book. Does it sound too good to be true? Take a look . . .

Premise

When everyone has gathered in one room, the mind reader announces that she would like to demonstrate a spectacular feat of psychic power. To begin, she selects three spectators to assist her in the experiment. The first one receives a sealed envelope, the second is given a book, and the third gets a slip of paper and a pencil.

The mind reader escorts this last spectator with the paper and pencil (let's call him the "writer") to the corner of the room so that he can concentrate, as his job is very important. To assist with the demonstration, the writer is asked to imagine opening a book to a random page. When he says he has reached the page in his mind, the performer asks him to note the page number and then write it down on his slip of paper.

The writer is now asked to mentally scan down the page he selected in his imaginary book and randomly select a line. Once he acknowledges that he has done this, he is to count how many lines down the page it is (in his mind), and then write that number on his slip of paper.

And finally, the writer is asked to randomly choose a word on that line. He doesn't have to see the word in his mind's eye; he only has to count the position of the word in the line. For example, the word all the way on the left of the line is #1, the word next to it is #2, and so forth. When he figures out the position of the word in the line, he writes that number on the same slip of paper.

Now that the numerical values of the page, line, and word have been written down, the writer folds up the paper and hands it to the mind reader. At this point in the trick, the spectator who is holding the book is invited to the front of the room. The mind reader hands the folded slip of paper to this spectator.

Can you see where this is going? The spectator is asked to open the slip of paper and then find the corresponding word in the book. So if the writer had written 178 for the page, 23 for the line, and 6 for the word, then the spectator holding the book would turn to page 178, count 23 lines down the page, and then identify the sixth word in the line. When he reaches this word, he is asked to announce it to the audience.

Now it's time to see what is inside the envelope that you handed to a spectator at the beginning of the demonstration. This spectator is called up to the front of the room and asked to open the envelope. He does so and removes an index card. Can you imagine the bedlam that will ensue when the audience sees that the word on the index card matches the word read out of the book?

Solution

First, let's bask in the wonder and, if you will allow me, stupefaction that you will surely inflict upon your audience with this spectacular stunt. It seems impossible, doesn't it? It appears as if you had predicted a word before starting the demonstration, and then somehow psychically willed a random member of the audience to mentally select the very same word. It's incomprehensible.

Incomprehensible, that is, until I let you in on the secret: Before beginning the demonstration, you select a book (any book will suffice) and thumb through until you find a word to your liking. You then take a slip of paper and write down the position of the word (page, line, and word). You fold this slip of paper and hide it in your hand. So when the writer hands you his slip of paper with the page, line, and word position, you secretly switch it with the one in your hand. You then hand the preset slip of paper to the volunteer holding the book.

So the slip of paper that you give to the spectator with the book is the one you had prepared ahead of time—and not the one that the writer handed you. And because you had planned the outcome ahead of time, you know that the word read by the spectator will indeed match the word in the envelope.

Tips & Techniques

The life of a mind reader is a stressful one. There are so many precautions to take, things to prepare, and risks to worry about. Page, Line, Word contains a few elements that may cause your blood pressure to rise.

The first concern is switching the slips of paper. In the context of this trick, the move is fairly simple and quick. An easy way to accomplish this is to conceal the fake slip of paper in your left hand. When the writer is ready to hand you his paper, take it in your right hand. Keep in mind—there is no rush to perform this maneuver. You do not have to make any hasty moves. When you feel comfortable and secure, casually put your hands together and pretend to take the real paper with your left hand. Then hand the fake slip of paper to the audience member with the book to present the conclusion.

61

Once the paper has been handed over, your job is to discreetly discard the writer's paper still in your hand. The best way to do this is wait until the audience's attention is on the person holding the book, and then nonchalantly slide your hand into your pocket. Mission accomplished . . . evidence eliminated from sight.

Of course, it would be more advantageous if you were able to switch the slips of paper in your hands. This way, you could slide the writer's paper in your pocket and then feel free to hold the fake slip of paper out in the open, waving it around confidently. After all, the switch has been made, and you have nothing to worry about. Well, almost nothing.

There is one other detail that needs to be addressed. If you do your job well, the audience will have no reason to suspect that the numbers on the slip of paper were phony. As a precaution, you should make sure that the writer and the person finding the word in the book do not speak to compare numbers when the trick has ended. If this should happen, your neat little scheme will unravel rapidly. I generally like to move on to another trick before the audience has a chance to investigate this possibility further.

Twenty-six

13

DIFFICULTY LEVEL: ✦✦✦✦✦
IMPACT: ✳✳✳✳✳
TECHNIQUE: MATHEMATICS
RISK: ✔✔✔✔✔

Overview

The difficulty level for this demonstration is a whopping three stars—but don't let that scare you off. It received three stars because there are so many steps to perform, not because it is difficult in any way. If you are able to count to 26, you have all the tools you need to pull it off. And because of some fun twists, this trick is a must for a mind reader's card trick repertoire.

Premise

The mind reader asks a spectator to shuffle a deck of cards until the audience is satisfied that the cards are random and the deck has not been preset. The spectator is then asked to look through the cards until she sees one that she likes. She then memorizes the card and whispers it to the other spectators. For good measure, the deck is shuffled again.

The mind reader takes the deck and examines the cards closely until he sees one that "seems to be communicating" with him. Let's assume this card was a **three of spades.** The mind reader puts the deck down, looks the spectator in the eye, and asks whether she selected the three of spades.

This, most likely, will not be correct, and the mind reader is at a loss how to proceed. After thinking for a moment, he comes up with an idea: He asks another spectator to take the *top third of the deck* and shuffle it like mad. Shuffle, shuffle, shuffle.

63

When this is done, the spectator is asked to replace the cards on top of the deck.

Then the original spectator is asked to look through the deck, find the card she selected, and then place it on top of the deck.

(See what I mean about there being a lot of steps to this one? Hang in there; we're almost through!)

And finally, one more spectator is asked to take the *bottom third of the deck* and shuffle it like mad. Shuffle, shuffle, shuffle. When this is completed, he then replaces the cards at the bottom of the deck. The mind reader then turns away and asks this spectator to cut the deck anywhere he likes. Now the mind reader is ready to use his superior mental talents to correctly identify the card.

Yes, many steps. But read below and you'll see how much fun this trick is to perform.

Solution

As a review, let's take a look at a brief summary of the trick. After you ask a spectator to mentally select a card, you look through the deck and offer a wild guess. After the audience tells you that you are wrong, the trick proceeds as follows.

Step 1: Top third of the deck is shuffled.
Step 2: Selected card is placed on top of the deck.
Step 3: Bottom third of the deck is shuffled.
Step 4: The deck is cut.
Step 5: The mind reader looks through the deck and finds the card.

Because of all the shuffling, the solution to this trick is so well hidden. Before I uncover the secret, let's take a look at *why* you have your spectators shuffling so much.

Remember, in Step 2, you have a spectator place her card on top of the deck. Well, if you had the top card memorized, then that would be a pretty easy trick to figure out, wouldn't it? All you would have to do is find the top card you memorized, and the spectator's card would be the next one behind it. So to remove this suspicion from the minds of the audience, you ask a spectator to shuffle the top third of the deck *before* the chosen card is placed on top. This way, if you had memorized the top card, it would have been completely lost in the shuffle.

But why have a spectator shuffle the bottom third? This is because in Step 4, you have a spectator cut the deck. Once the deck is cut, the bottom card and the top card would be right next to each other. And it wouldn't take very long for someone to suspect that you had memorized the bottom card. So, again, to remove this suspicion from the minds of your paranoid audience, have a spectator shuffle the bottom third of the deck—to guarantee that you did not memorize the bottom card.

See? I'm not as crazy as you had originally suspected.

So, if you don't memorize the top card, and you don't memorize the bottom card, how on earth are you supposed to know which card has been selected? Easy: *Memorize the middle card.* Come again? Yes, the middle card. Here's how:

At the beginning of the trick when you first looked through the deck to find a card that "communicated" to you? Well, what you were actually doing was *counting through the deck to find the twenty-sixth card from the top.* Just remember, if you count from the bottom, memorize the twenty-seventh card since that will be the twenty-sixth card from the top. The reason that this is significant is because when the spectator places her card on top of the deck, the card you memorized will be 26 cards from it (possibly 27, but see Tips & Techniques for a way around that).

Even though the top and bottom thirds of the deck were shuffled like mad, this did not disturb the position of the twenty-sixth card. And the fact that the deck was cut still does not change the fact that the spectator's card is 26 (possibly 27) cards from the card that you memorized.

So all you have to do to conclude this trick is to look through the deck, locate the card you memorized, and then count off 26 cards to find the spectator's card.

Tips & Techniques

To me, the most fun part of this trick is seeing *the look* on the spectators' faces. Do you know which look I mean?

I usually like to start the trick by making an outlandish claim. I state that my mind-reading talents are so powerful, so limitless, that if someone in the room looked through a well-shuffled deck of cards and randomly memorized one, I would be able to announce what it was. And then I continue: "And it's not only because I am a great mind reader; it is because *I am a great person as well.* And I intend to prove my greatness with a little demonstration."

Of course, the smug observers usually snicker and make rude comments, such as: "You can barely tie your own shoelaces. How are you going to pick the right card?" To this I generally reply, "Oh, you little, weak people. Just sit back and watch my amazing talents in action."

Then I begin the trick. After an intense shuffle-fest (audiences really love to shuffle cards), I ask a spectator to look through the deck and mentally select one. Then I scan through the cards (to count to the twenty-sixth card and memorize it). When I am done, I put the deck on the table, stand up, and announce, "Prepare to be flabbergasted, my skeptical audience. Prepare to bow to me and acknowledge my greatness—as a mind reader and as a human being." I then make a wild guess at the card.

And with the odds being 1 in 52, my wild guess is usually very, very wrong. That, my mind-reading friends, is when I get to see *the look.* After I announced my greatness over and over, everyone in the room witnesses me being wrong. Dead wrong. The look of smugness, mixed with gloating and a sprinkle of "ha-ha-I-told-you-so-you're-not-as-great-as-you-think-you-are" spreads on the spectators' faces. And I stand there, pretending to be a broken, crushed, and humiliated mentalist. Oh, how I love that look. Because in a matter of moments, their worlds will be shattered when they realize that I was merely luring them into a false sense of superiority.

And consider this: Statistically speaking, 1 out of every 52 times you perform this trick, your wild guess will actually be correct! Can you imagine the *horror* that your audience will experience? I mean, think about what happened: Someone looked through the deck and mentally memorized a card—and you were able to name it. The only conclusion they could come to is that you must have made some sort of deal with the devil. Well, let me tell you, if you should ever be so fortunate as to name the correct card at this stage of the trick, pack your bags, pawn your mind-reading gear, and quit the business for good. Because you will never be able to top the miracle you just performed.

But, alas, this only works 1 in 52 times, and this type of luck has never graced itself upon me—despite more than a hundred tries. So we're going to have to find the answer the hard way—and that means trickery and deception.

After you make your wild guess, be sure that someone in the audience doesn't blurt out the name of the card. You don't want to hear, "Wrong, wise guy, it was the six of clubs," since that would end the trick before you had a chance to do your magic. To prevent this from happening, try phrasing your question in a yes-or-no format: "Was your card the three of clubs?" And when the spectator says no, immediately enter into the next phase, letting the audience know that the trick is not over yet.

When you think about it, the only thing you have to do is memorize the twenty-sixth card from the top. Once you do that, the rest of the trick is practically foolproof. But there is one very important fact that I have to tell you. It's more of a snag, really—but nothing to panic about!

There is a 50 percent chance that the spectator's card will be 27 cards past your secret card, and not 26. This is because when the spectator retrieves his card and places it at the top, he may pull it out from the bottom half of the deck. This would then put his card 27 away from your secret card instead of 26. But is this a reason for you to freak out? Not at all, my easily panicked mind-reading chum. Here is what you do:

When you find your secret card, silently count through the deck to find the spectator's card. When you reach the 26th card, place it on the top of the deck. Then place the 27th card on the bottom of the deck. Make sure you take note of both cards. Your job is then to find the biggest difference between the cards and ask the audience one question.

Here is an example: Let's say that the cards were a **queen of spades** and a **four of diamonds.** You will ask, "Please tell me one thing: Was the card you chose black or red?" Once the audience answers this, you know which card to present. And it will look like you knew all along, because you will either be showing the top card or the bottom card.

Sometimes the cards are the same color, so you may have to ask a different question, such as:

Was it a spade?

Was it a picture card?

Was it an odd or even number?

In each case, look for a difference between the cards, and ask your audience a question so you can be sure of your selection. You can eliminate this dilemma altogether if you simply watch to see from where in the deck the spectator takes the card. If you see her pulling it from the top half of the deck, stick with the twenty-sixth card; conversely, if she takes her card from the bottom half, count off to the twenty-seventh card.

Presenting the Finish

As always, you have the option of ending the demonstration quickly and simply flashing the correct card to the audience. But that may leave you feeling incomplete and unsatisfied. May I suggest a couple of alternatives?

Before revealing the card: If the spectator's card is on the bottom of the deck, make sure that you wave the cards around as you speak, giving everyone in the room a chance to see that the card is on the bottom. Then, from the top of the deck, start to deal several cards face up onto the table. After seven or eight cards have been turned over, grab ahold of the next card, and before turning it over, announce to the audience: "After a momentary lapse, I have felt my greatness return. And this time, it's back with a vengeance. I can honestly say that I am now greater than I have ever been in my entire life. I am willing to wager anything that *the very next card I turn over* will be the correct card. Do any of you dare to bet against my greatness?"

Well, there you are with your hand poised on the next top card, and everyone in the room has seen that the selected card is on the bottom of the deck! Not only that; you have already proven that you are an utterly incompetent mind reader—having messed up once earlier in the trick. It is likely that a good portion of your audience would be willing to bet that you will mess up again.

And that is when you get to have the last laugh. After all bets have been made, you sneakily reach under the deck, grab the bottom card, and flip it over onto the table. The very next card you turned over was, indeed, the correct card.

What happens if the spectator's card is on top of the deck? That's just as easy. As you are dealing cards onto the table, your audience will see the top card being turned over, and will assume that you have passed it by for good. After bets have been made, retrieve the correct card and flip it over on the table.

Don't Try This at Home

I hesitate to tell you this next idea, because it is a recipe for disaster. You bought (found? stole?) this book because it contains *easy* mind-reading tricks. This idea for presenting the finish is anything but easy. In fact, it takes courage, skill, and a little stupidity to even try it. You have been cautioned. Here it is:

Once you find out which card has been selected, make sure you place it on top of the deck. You will have a few pieces of folded-over Scotch tape hidden in your hand (the tape is rolled in a circle with the sticky side out). Press the deck into your hand firmly, making sure that the little Scotch tape balls transfer from your hand to the top card.

With me so far? Good, because here is where it gets bizarre. Start to act very frustrated. Pace around the room mumbling about how nothing ever works out for you. You try and you try, but you can never get anything right. Ah, how you wish you never became a mind reader in the first place. You should have become an accountant like your parents wanted. And so on. By this point, your blood is boiling, and you are practically in tears. In an act of utter desperation, you let out a yell and throw (yes, throw!) the deck of cards against the wall. And then . . . and then . . . silence.

The audience is shocked to see that *the chosen card is sticking to the wall!* Could you imagine a more dramatic finish? Of course not, because there isn't any. But be warned: Unless you practice this thoroughly, you will end up in a most undignified manner, crawling around the floor searching for a card with Scotch tape on the back.

The Evil King

DIFFICULTY LEVEL: ✦✦✦✦✦
IMPACT: ✳✳✳✳✳
TECHNIQUES: MATHEMATICS/PRESET CARDS
RISK: ✔✔✔✔✔

Overview

Blast that Evil King. He's foiled me too many times. The only way to put an end to his diabolical powers is to remove him from the deck altogether. This is another trick that relies on the number 26 to demonstrate your psychic abilities.

Premise

The mind reader explains to the audience that ever since playing cards were invented in February of 1987, the Evil King has plagued mind readers, mentalists, and psychics like no other card in the deck. In a paranoid frenzy, the mind reader searches through the deck and removes the offending card.

The mind reader takes the remaining 51 cards and holds them to his forehead. Once his psychic powers kick in, he puts the deck on the table and frantically scribbles a prediction on a slip of paper. He seals his prediction in an envelope and places it on the table next to the cards.

A volunteer is asked to remove a small portion of cards from the top of the deck while the mind reader is not looking. Once this is accomplished, the mind reader then counts off half the deck in a pile on the table. And how much is half the deck? 26 cards, exactly. So picture this: There is now a stack of 26 cards on the table, and a small packet of cards held by the spectator. The remaining cards are put aside (they are not necessary).

The mind reader then asks the spectator to count the cards he removed from the deck. For the sake of this explanation, let's assume that the spectator took 10 cards. He is then instructed to remove the same number of cards (10) off the top of the pile that the mind reader laid out on the table.

Now, the mind reader asks another spectator to turn over the top card so that everyone in the room can see it. Let's assume that the card is a **four of diamonds.**

Remember that prediction you made at the beginning of the trick? Well, now would be a great time to reveal it. Have one last spectator unseal the envelope, pull out the slip of paper, and read your prediction aloud. Wouldn't it be amazing if the prediction matched the top card? Of course it would! Read the solution to see how you can make this happen.

Solution

It's our friend mathematics at work again, casting its dark powers upon your unsuspecting audience. All you have to do is memorize the twenty-sixth card and the trick practically performs itself.

And how will you identify the twenty-sixth card? That's the best part of the trick. All that nonsense about the Evil King was merely a clever ruse to allow you to rifle through the deck and count to the twenty-sixth card.

This is the card that you will identify on the slip of paper and seal in the envelope. Let's review the rest of the trick:

1. A spectator removes a small portion of cards from the top of the deck.
2. The mind reader takes the deck and counts off 26 cards onto a table.
3. The spectator counts his cards and then removes that same amount from the top of the deck on the table.
4. Another spectator turns over the top card.
5. The envelope is opened to see that the prediction matches the card.

But how? What does the twenty-sixh card have to do with anything? Is it too late to return this book? You pose some very good questions. Let's see whether I can answer them one at a time.

71

Let's say that the twenty-sixth card is the **four of diamonds;** so you write this as your prediction. The deck of cards is sitting on the table minding its own business. You ask a spectator to remove a small packet of cards from the top. We will assume that he took 10 cards (whatever amount of cards he takes won't change the outcome of the trick).

So now that the spectator took 10 cards, where is the **four of diamonds?** Well, since it was 26 cards down, and the spectator took 10 cards off the pile, it will now be 16 cards down.

So far, so good? Okay, stay with me . . .

You now pick up the deck and count 26 cards onto the table. You can pile these cards one on top of another until you reach the twenty-sixth card. Then put the other cards aside. So now you have 26 cards on the table. And since the **four of diamonds** was the sixteenth card, *there will now be 10 cards on top of it.*

Do you see where this is going? The spectator then counts his pile of cards (10) and removes that same number from the top of the deck. And what happens when 10 cards are removed? *That leaves the* **four of diamonds** *as the top card!*

Then all you have to do is have a spectator turn it over and it will match the prediction in your envelope.

Tips & Techniques

In our example, we said that the spectator took 10 cards off the top of the deck. But what if he took another number instead? Would the trick work just as well?

The answer is yes. You don't believe me? Okay, let's try it with 15:

The spectator lifts 15 cards from the top of the deck. This means that the four of diamonds is 11 cards down. When you count out 26 cards on the table, the four of diamonds will have 15 cards on top of it. And when the spectator removes 15 cards from the top of the deck, the top card will again be the four of diamonds.

Mathematically, no matter how many cards the spectator decides to take off the top of the deck, when the trick is over, the top card will *always* be your original 26th card.

An important note! People have a tendency to count from the bottom of the deck when the cards are facing them. If you do this, you must remember to count to the *twenty-seventh card* instead—because when you flip the deck back over that will be the one that is 26 down. Does that make sense? Try it and you'll see what I mean.

Oh, and try not to forget to remove a king from the deck (since that's the reason that you said that you were looking through the deck in the first place!). Make sure that the king you remove is from the bottom half of the deck (this way it doesn't affect the twenty-sixth card you memorized). Once you practice a couple of times, it will seem like second nature to you.

What makes this trick seem so remarkable is that the spectator is at liberty to choose how large a stack he removes from the deck. You should emphasize this fact to the audience when the trick is finished. Remind them that no one forced your spectator to remove 10 cards. He could have chosen 0 or 10 or anything in between. He selected a stack of 10 cards freely. And, as a mind reader, you knew that's how many he was going to select, which is why you were able to figure out the top card in advance.

What if the spectator removes more than 26 cards? Well, then the trick is ruined. But keep in mind that you asked him to remove a *small* packet of cards. People generally lift between 5 and 15 cards from the deck.

15

Mystical Memory

DIFFICULTY LEVEL: ◆◆◆◆◆
IMPACT: ✳✳✳✳✳ (WARM-UP)
TECHNIQUE: OUTRIGHT DECEIT
RISK: ✔✔✔✔✔

Overview

As mind readers, we get away with so much. And I'm not talking about only the shenanigans we pull when we pretend to read someone's thoughts. I am referring to the nonsense that we tell our audiences in order to add credibility and mystery to our mind-reading demonstrations.

In Mystical Memory, we have yet another opportunity to provide our audience with more made-up facts about mind reading and mysticism. "It is a well-known fact in mind reading circles," you can say, standing in front of the room gesturing grandly as if you are an attorney delivering your opening statement to a jury. "It is a well-known fact that mind-reading talent and a strong memory go hand in hand. It is rare, indeed, that you will find a gifted mind reader who cannot perform remarkable feats of memorization." And to prove it, you perform the following:

Premise

Having proclaimed his superior memorization talents, the mind reader stands in front of the audience holding the sports section of a newspaper. He says that he is going to read off a list of baseball scores and asks a spectator to write down what he says.

After reading about 20 numbers (more, if you like), the mind reader stops, folds up the newspaper, and puts it aside. He makes a few more remarks about the difficulty associated with memorizing large groups of numbers. When the audience agrees that it would indeed be a spectacular feat of mental powers to be able to recall all 20 scores that were just read, it's time to conclude the demonstration.

With utmost concentration, a few distorted faces, and several awkward grunts, the mind reader proceeds to recite each one of the numbers he read a few moments ago—in the same order. And since a spectator wrote down each score, he can verify that the numbers match exactly.

Is it really possible to instantly memorize 20 or more numbers and then recite them back moments later? Perhaps. But the better question is: *Is memorization even necessary?*

Solution

No, it's not necessary to memorize all those numbers on the spot. This is because *you already have these numbers memorized.* When you open the newspaper to the sports page, you won't actually read back the real baseball scores. Instead, you will say numbers that you already know. Do you have a social security number? An account number that you've memorized? An old telephone number? Most people have several personal numbers already memorized. All you have to do is pretend that these numbers are the baseball scores. So, what appears to be a remarkable demonstration of mental ability is nothing more than you rattling off a few personal numbers.

Tips & Techniques

Your acting ability will make or break this trick. Since the audience thinks that you are reading baseball scores out of the newspaper, then you must appear as if you are reading and not reciting numbers that you have memorized. This can be done by pausing after each two numbers, pretending to lose your place once in a while, and scanning all over the page as if you are searching for more scores. Make sure that you explain to one of the spectators the importance of writing down each score as you call it off.

Because no one knows my social security number, I generally start with that, followed by my bank account number, and then my driver's license number.

If the audience insists upon looking at the newspaper to verify your scores when the trick is over, tell them you read the scores in no particular order, only to ensure that it was all random. This way they will be unable to match the scores with the numbers you read.

It is more effective if you prolong the demonstration and banter a while before presenting the conclusion. This way, you are putting extra time between reading the scores and reciting them back, making it appear even more spectacular.

If you prefer, you can use horseracing results, stock prices, or any other numbers instead of baseball scores. You can even use playing cards (just the number, not the suit). If you use cards, make sure that you give them a quick shuffle as soon as you finish reading off the numbers.

A Great Variation

Want to punch up the impact level of this trick a notch? Well, if you do, you will have to also increase the level of difficulty. Up for it?

Instead of reading baseball scores from a newspaper, you can read a list of names from a book, magazine, newspaper, or any other publication that is handy. This variation becomes more challenging because now you have to come up with a list of people instead of numbers. Do you know a group of people that you could recite off the top of your head? Perhaps the first names of players on a baseball team? Do you know the first names of the first dozen or so U.S. presidents? (Probably not, but it would be easy enough to learn.) If you are performing this stunt for people you do not know well, then members of your family (in age order) can be used.

As in the prior version, the order of the names is important. Will it still be an impressive feat if you can recite all 20 names, but out of sequence? Yes; but it will be much more so if you list the names in the order they were first read.

16

Pick a Card, Any Card

DIFFICULTY LEVEL: ✦✦✦✦✦
IMPACT: ✹✹✹✹✹ OR ✹✹✹✹✹ (DEPENDING ON PRESENTATION)
TECHNIQUE: SLEIGHT OF HAND
RISK: ✔✔✔✔✔

Overview

In its simplest form, the trick is a breeze to perform, and it consistently receives a strong audience response. If, however, you are willing to toss dignity to the wind and act like a complete lunatic, then this demonstration provides you with the opportunity to give a memorable performance.

Premise

The mind reader fans out a deck of cards and has a spectator "pick a card, any card." The spectator selects one and shows it to the other members of the audience; then places it back in the deck. The mind reader is able to look through the deck and pull out the correct card.

Solution

What a cliché. How many times have you seen a magician fan out a deck of cards and say "Pick a card, any card"?

What makes this trick different is the presentation. You will be using your "mental powers" to penetrate the skulls of your audience and determine the right card. But before we get to that, allow me to reveal this extremely simple solution.

After a volunteer has selected a card, she is instructed to show it to the rest of the audience, making sure that the mind reader does not see it. While the audience is busy looking at the chosen card, you do something very sneaky. You flip the deck over in your hand. Just flip that sucker right over. Now the deck is *face up* in your hand. You then take the top card and *turn it over.* This way, all of the cards in your hand are face up—except for the very top card, which is face down. So when the audience sees the deck in your hand, they will think that all of the cards are face down.

All you have to do is ask the spectator to slide the card back into the deck—anywhere she wants. But! You must make sure to hold the deck in your hand in a stack, not fanned out. Did you just ask why? It's so that the audience doesn't find out that all of the other cards are face up!

Now that the card has been placed back in the deck, your task of identifying the correct card becomes much simpler. *It's the only card in the deck that's face down!* (Except for the top card, which you turned over.)

 ## Tips & Techniques

First, let's address the technical part of the demonstration. To execute this trick properly, you need to perform a simple sleight of hand maneuver. As the spectators pass the selected card around, you have a perfect opportunity to turn the deck over. Everyone will be looking at the spectator's card and will not notice when you casually turn the deck over in your hand. As soon as you flip the deck, turn over the top card and then you are ready. Be sure not to rush this move. The only way you will get caught is if you fumble with the cards in haste. When everyone present has seen the selected card, you are ready to continue.

Once the spectator has replaced the card in the deck, your job is to rifle through the deck and find the one card that is facing the wrong way. There is a very simple and straightforward way of accomplishing this.

While casually bantering with the audience, hold the cards facing you and rapidly *thumb* through the deck until you see the card that is facing the wrong way. While the deck still faces you, move the spectator's card to the top and then subtly sneak a peek at it. If you practice this a few times, you will see that it is very easy to do.

If, however, these moves make you uneasy, here are some alternative methods of flipping the deck and finding the card:

You could turn around for a moment and do your dirty work with your back to the audience. Keep in mind that this is equivalent to saying, "Hello, audience! I'm doing something very sneaky here—bear with me a moment while I pull a fast one on you." They may not know exactly what you are up to, but their suspicions will certainly be aroused.

Start with a deck of cards in its case. Then after someone picks a card, replace the cards back into the case—but *face up.* When the spectator replaces the card in the deck, he will naturally do so face down. If you use this variation, you won't have to worry about flipping over the top card. Then remove the cards from the case and locate the correct card.

In any case, you must make it clear that the spectator has complete freedom in replacing the card in the deck. It would be best if you looked away while this was being done so that the audience doesn't suspect you of knowing where the card was placed.

An Entertaining Finish

On the surface, this appears to be just another "pick a card, any card" trick that everyone has seen countless times. But you can turn this ho-hum card trick into a wacky mind-reading exhibition with some showmanship.

After you have scanned through the deck and determined which card was selected, it is time for you to demonstrate your superhuman psychic powers and reveal the card to the audience. For the sake of this demonstration, let's assume that the chosen card was the **queen of diamonds.**

At this point in the demonstration, I start to act frustrated, as if I can't seem to focus on the answer. I apologize to the audience and say that something in the air must be blocking my powers. I tell them that I can reveal the answer if I go directly to the source. What do I mean by that? One word: *Phrenology.*

I enjoy making up ridiculous scientific reasons to explain my mind-reading ability. Phrenology is the science of analyzing the shape of a person's skull and the bumps in it to find out things about his or her character. I tell my audience that this branch of science was invented by two German doctors in the early 1800s (which, by the way, is true). I then state that I am able to use this scientific technology to find out what a person is thinking.

Will people actually let you use phrenology to read their thoughts? Usually. Have a spectator sit in a chair and ask her to concentrate on the chosen card. Make sure she pictures the image of the card in her mind. As she does, place both hands on her head and start to feel the bumps. After a few seconds, you can say, "Yes, I'm starting to get a signal . . . Yes . . . Make sure to pick up bread on the way home . . . I wonder if there is any pie left . . ." Take your hands off her head and say, "I thought I told you to concentrate on your card! We will try it again; only this time, think of the card, please."

As you resume your position with your hands on her head, put on your most serious face—as if you are mentally searching through her thoughts. All of a sudden, you are struck with a stream of energy from her brain, through her skull, into your hands, and up to your brain. Your eyes bulge as you say, "It's a picture card . . ."

You then quickly move to the next spectator and start to feel the bumps on his head. If you prefer, you can tell the audience what some of his random thoughts are. At some point you will be overwhelmed by his brain pattern. You immediately stiffen and say, "It's a red card!"

Moving across the room, you analyze the bumps on another spectator's skull until you shout out, "A diamond!"

By now you are feeling mentally drained from sucking the thoughts out of the heads of your audience (even Spock needed a nap after an intense Vulcan mind-meld). But you aren't finished yet. You have already revealed that it is a red picture card. You then stated that it is a diamond. But now it's time to go to one last spectator and announce the card.

Place your hands firmly on her head. Breathe deeply . . . focus . . . stiffen . . . tremble wildly . . . and then with your remaining energy, blurt out, "It's a queen . . . yes! The **queen of diamonds!**" Your hands fall from her head as you collapse in a chair, watching the stunned faces of your audience.

That is all you would need to do to let your audience know that: (1) you are a serious mind reader; and (2) you are truly deranged. But, if you want to really go over the top to present this trick, you could tell the audience about the *psychograph.* A psychograph was a machine that was invented in the early 1900s to read people's thoughts. The first machine, introduced in 1931, contained almost 2,000 parts. But more than seven decades later, you have developed a simplified version that works just as well.

You then produce a helmet or hat that you dug out from your closet or picked up at a flea market. To make it look "authentic," you can attach bells or wires or phone cords—or any other decoration you deem appropriate for mind reading. Instead of feeling your spectators' heads, you can have them wear your psychograph while you hold the other end of the phone cord to your ear. Not even the most gullible spectators will believe in your contraption, but when you identify the correct card, they will certainly wonder, *How did you do that??*

Little Napkin Balls

DIFFICULTY LEVEL: ✦✦✦✦✦
IMPACT: ✳✳✳✳✳ (OH, YES!)
TECHNIQUE: ONE AHEAD/SWITCHING
RISK: ✔✔✔✔✔

Overview

Because of the personal nature of this mind-blowing demonstration, I prefer performing it for an audience of one. The impact is so powerful that many people actually get scared when they see it. And if you are performing it for someone who happens to believe in mysticism, the paranormal, and ESP, then you will have her convinced that you are indeed psychic.

One of the best features of Little Napkin Balls is that it is a perfect demonstration to perform impromptu when someone challenges you to prove your mystical powers.

Premise

The mind reader sits across a table from his victim—I mean, subject—and hands her three napkin strips. These strips are torn from any ordinary napkin and are approximately one inch long and two inches wide. The mind reader asks his subject to write down three questions that she wants answered—one on each napkin strip—and then to roll the napkins into little balls. She then places the three napkin balls on the table.

The mind reader asks his subject to pick up one of the little napkin balls and place it on her head. As she does, the mind reader concentrates until he envisions the answer to the question written on the napkin ball. When he has answered her question, he then repeats the same miracle with the other two napkin balls in the same fashion.

Little Napkin Balls isn't only fun to say; when performed correctly, it packs an amazing punch.

Solution

The One Ahead Principle is one of the most effective mind-reading techniques ever invented. It has been used by psychics and other sneaky people for generations. Once you know *just one* of the answers, you are able to name all three. To understand how this principle can be applied to Little Napkin Balls, let's run through the demonstration in more detail.

As I mentioned, you start by handing your subject three napkin strips. What I didn't say is that you actually have four napkin strips. Before the demonstration begins, you will have already rolled up this fourth napkin strip into a tight ball and hidden it in your hand. And to ensure that you will be able to recognize the fake napkin ball later, you twist the end so it has a little tail on it.

You then give your subject her instructions: One at a time, she is to write a question on a napkin strip, roll it into a ball, and place it on the table. When she is about to begin, you walk away from the table to give her privacy. It cannot appear that you have even the slightest opportunity to peer over and peek at what she is writing.

You return to the table when she is in the process of rolling her third, and last, napkin ball. As you approach the table, you stop her and say, "No, no, no, a *tight* ball. Let me show you." You take the ball from her and, under the guise of tightening her napkin ball, you *switch it with the one hidden in your hand.* This move is extremely simple to master and takes a split second to execute. (See Tips & Techniques for guidance.)

So now there are three napkin balls sitting on the table in front of your subject. Two of them contain questions she wrote, and the last is the fake one that you had planted. In your hand is one of the napkin balls with a question on it.

You ask the subject to take the three napkin balls in front of her, shake them up in her hands, and place them back on the table. You then push one of the napkin balls toward her and ask her to place it on her head and concentrate. Obviously, you must push one of the balls with a question written on it—not the fake one with a tail! While she is doing this, your hands are busy below the table opening the little napkin ball you have stolen. Ask her whether she is focusing on her questions. When she answers yes, you bow your head slightly, as if you are trying to summon your powers.

Once you have glimpsed her question, you then proceed to piece together an answer. For the sake of this explanation, let's assume that her question was *Will I get a promotion at work this year?* Here is one way you may choose to answer:

"I sense that this question has something to do with business or your job. In my mind's eye, I can see you in the workplace speaking with your boss, being complimented on a job well done. I see you shaking hands . . . smiling. And now I see you being moved into a bigger office. I'm not sure what your question was, but it seems as if you're asking about something that will happen at your job."

As her eyes bulge out of her sockets in disbelief, you ask her to hand you the napkin ball that was on her head. You open it and nod, as if it all makes sense now. You say, "Oh, I see. You wanted to know if you were going to get a promotion this year. Well, if my premonition is any indication, it looks quite favorable!"

Do you see what you've just done? She handed you the napkin ball that she was holding (thinking, of course, that it contained the question about her job). But when you open this napkin ball,

84

you will be able to sneak a peek at the next question. So with this information, you push another napkin ball toward your subject and ask her to place it on her head. You then go through the same routine in answering her second and third questions.

When you have finished answering all three questions, you will be in possession of all four napkin balls. All you have to do is place the three real balls back on the table while hiding the fourth out of sight or in your pocket.

Tips & Techniques

This demonstration is powerful on two levels. In the first place, you are able to magically identify the questions that the subject secretly writes on the napkin strips. But more significant is that it appears as if you contacted the spirits to find the *answers* to her questions.

As you already read in the solution, it's best if you seem not to know the exact wording of the question. This makes it look much more authentic that the answer was somehow mystically being communicated to you.

Before you run out and try this cruel trick on your family and closest friends, let's first discuss the technical part—the sleight of hand. Picture the scene: You are standing away from the table as you watch your subject roll up her third napkin ball. You walk over and, seeing that she is rolling the napkin incorrectly, demonstrate how it's supposed to be done. Follow these steps:

- Walk over with the fake napkin ball hidden in your *left* hand.
- Pick up her napkin ball with your *right* hand as you say, "No, a *tight* ball."
- Press her napkin ball into your left hand and switch it with the fake napkin ball. While you are pretending to scrunch up the napkin tightly, it will be ridiculously easy for you to make the switch undetected.
- Place the fake napkin ball with the tail on the table with the other two.
- Walk back to your seat with the subject's napkin ball hidden in your left hand.

The only way you can mess up the switch is if you are overly dramatic in the execution. There is no need to strenuously twist the paper in your hand until veins bulge from your neck. Take your time. You only have to appear as if you are twisting the napkin tighter; this requires only a modest effort and should take about a second to complete.

Once the switch has been made, the only tricky part is opening the napkin and reading what is written on it. The reason that this demonstration uses napkins instead of paper is because napkins make less noise when you're unscrunching them.

If you follow these directions, you will be able to pull this off flawlessly every time. At this point in the trick, you will see three napkin balls on the table. Gently and casually push one of the balls to the subject (obviously, *not* the one with the tail) and ask her to place it on her head. If you prefer, she can hold it to her forehead.

While you are telling her what to do, your hands are below the surface of the table where she can't see them, slowly opening the napkin ball. You ask her to concentrate on her questions. While she concentrates, lower your head for a moment and *glance* at the question. Did you read what I just wrote? I wrote *glance*. I didn't write "stare at" or "fixate upon." I wrote *glance*. There's nothing that will ruin this trick faster than a mind reader who makes it obvious that he's reading something under the table—even worse if his lips move while he's reading it. Just *glance* at it. Have I made my point?

If, when you glance down, you see that the napkin was upside down or turned the wrong way, you should look away, adjust the paper and glance down again. As always, do not rush this move—you will have time.

If you like, you can even ask your subject to cover up the other two napkin balls with her hand and then close her eyes while she concentrates. If she agrees, you have even less to worry about. But does this mean that you then have permission to stare and gape at the napkin? No—just *glance*. As I always say, you can never count on a mind-reading subject to keep her eyes closed.

You will find it helpful if you insist that your subject write her answers as clearly as possible. You can explain that the psychic gods are quite old and have trouble reading bad handwriting.

There is a potentially difficult situation that may arise during this performance. Sometimes the subject takes this experiment quite seriously. She will write three questions that have major importance to her. This is especially true with people who have a tendency to believe in the paranormal. If this is the case, you must answer the questions delicately.

You may see a question like *Will Uncle Dave survive his operation on Thursday?* It is a cruel mind reader indeed who answers that question with "I see a tragic death in your family this coming week." This is especially true if you've already answered the first two questions for her, and she is convinced that you really are psychic. I would be vague and say something like: "I see that there is an important event happening to a family member in the coming week. And I see everyone in the family rallying, giving all of their support and love. This will help his chances considerably." If she hates Uncle Dave, however, then she won't be too happy with your interpretation.

18

The Trusting Mentalist

DIFFICULTY LEVEL: ◆◆◆◆◆
IMPACT: ✳✳✳✳✳
TECHNIQUES: UNWITTING COLLUSION/PRAYER
RISK: ✔✔✔✔✔ (YIKES!) CODE RED/BEWARE/RUN FOR THE HILLS

Overview

I warn you—if you have a weak stomach or cannot handle a *high-risk* demonstration, then skip this chapter. Forget you ever laid your eyes upon it. In fact, rip the next few pages out of the book so you won't be able to succumb to the temptation of reading it. In The Trusting Mentalist, the danger of getting caught is REAL!

Having given you fair warning, I now feel comfortable saying that this is one of my all-time favorite demonstrations to perform. I used an established technique to create a high-impact psychic exhibition. Here is my version of this very daring trick . . .

Premise

The mind reader asks the audience to select two people to participate in a mind-reading experiment. Each participant is asked to secretly write down a date from history and seal it in an envelope. The mind reader also writes a date from history and seals it in a third envelope.

The three envelopes are then given to three other spectators. One by one, the envelopes are opened and the dates are read aloud. And get this: *All three dates match.* Okay, catch your breath, stop shaking your head, and learn how you can make this happen.

Solution

First, I'd like you to think of the impact this exhibition will have on your audience when they see that you matched the date of both participants. Is it worth taking a substantial risk to accomplish such an amazing feat? If you'd enjoy seeing the stunned faces of your audience as the dates are revealed, then the answer should be *yes!* Of course, I'll show you how to minimize your risk of getting caught.

After seeing this demonstration performed, the audience will at first suspect that the two participants are conspirators and have been in cahoots with the mind reader since the beginning. Well, this is only partly correct. You see, *the two participants were selected by the audience.* The mind reader had absolutely no control over who was selected for this trick. So, how could he have conspired with the participants if he had no idea whom the audience was going to choose for the experiment?

Here's how (get ready to scream *"Are you out of your mind-reading mind??"*):

Let me set up the scenario so you can see exactly how this will play out. You are in a room with at least 5 spectators (I generally prefer 25 to 50 observers for this feat). While everyone is seated, you talk to your audience about psychic exhibitions. After explaining how you are able to psychically transmit thoughts to anyone you choose, you propose to prove it in an intense mind-reading experiment.

First, you ask the audience to nominate two volunteers. Tell the audience to be sure to select two people who they believe are definitely not in collaboration with you. After these two volunteers have been selected, you invite the first one to join you at the front of the room. You then ask the audience whether they are 100-percent confident that this person has not been in cahoots with you. "If there is any doubt whatsoever," you can say, "then please replace this person with someone else. I want you to be *absolutely certain* that the people you select are innocent of any preplanning with me." You then go through the same process with the second volunteer.

Wow, that's pretty powerful, don't you think? The audience has full control over whether or not to keep or exchange this person. So how could you POSSIBLY have rigged the experiment ahead of time? It hardly seems likely.

Now that the two volunteers have been declared safe by the audience, it is time to conduct the experiment. You position the two participants at a safe distance from each other and hand both of them several index cards and an envelope.

You instruct them to write a date on their index cards—any date in history. What do I mean by any date? Well, what I mean is *any date.* It can be yesterday, or two weeks ago, or July 4, 1776, or March 31, 5005 B.C. Get it? *Any date at all.*

But ask them to write this date on three separate index cards. On the first card, they will write the month. The second card will have the day of the month, and the last card is for the year. Tell them to place the cards in the envelope in that order when they have finished.

Here is the part where you have to keep your fingers crossed; where you have to pray that everything goes as planned; where you have to trust in the indecency of humankind. This is because when you hand your volunteers their index cards, they will each see a yellow sticky note on top that says:

"I'm counting on you! Please write down December 6, 1805. It's our secret. Shhh! And act surprised!"

I assume that half of you reading this have just ripped the book in half and tossed it out of your limousine window. Fine; be that way. Go on eating your caviar and sipping your fancy martinis—forget you ever heard about mind reading in the first place. But for the other half of you who are still reading, I offer the following Tips & Techniques to help you through this trick.

Tips & Techniques

How dare I, you ask? How dare I suggest that you put yourself in such a position? I share your concern. But let me start off by saying that this trick *usually* works flawlessly. Are you worried that the volunteers will tell the audience what you have done and read the secret notes aloud to everyone in the room—causing you much humiliation and angst? Surprisingly, that is not the biggest risk of this trick. On the rare occasions when I have been busted performing this demonstration it has been because the volunteers' reactions gave it away.

Instead of acting naturally, sometimes volunteers have a tendency of tipping their hands by giggling or reacting in a noticeable way. Here is how I combat this unfortunate possibility:

- I place the index cards and yellow sticky notes inside each envelope before handing it to the volunteers.
- I tell them not to look in the packet until I give them the signal.
- After instructing them about writing a date on their index cards, I tell them to look in their packets.
- I then immediately tend to the task of distracting the audience.

I move to a different part of the room—making sure all spectators' eyes are on me—and I proceed to educate the audience in the history of mind reading:

"Although psychic experiments have been around for quite some time, the first documented use of mind reading was by the French magician Jean Eugene Robert-Houdin. Born in 1805, he was regarded as one of the finest magicians of the nineteenth century. Dubbed 'The Father of Modern Magic,' Robert-Houdin enjoyed including his son in some of his routines. In a famous mind-reading exhibition, Robert-Houdin brought his son up to the stage and blindfolded him. He then walked into the audience and asked a spectator to give him a personal object (a watch, wallet, key, etc.). Robert-Houdin would then ring a bell, at which point his son would identify the object. Of course, some people at the time suspected that Robert-Houdin used the bell to transmit signals to his son, but we know today that it was real magic."

At this point in my fascinating story, the two volunteers would have finished writing their dates on the index cards and secured them in their envelopes. I then ask the volunteers to hand their envelopes to two other spectators in the audience.

Before concluding the exhibition, I announce that I, too, will write a date on three index cards and place them in another envelope. After completing this task, I give my envelope to a random spectator.

The Grand Finale

It is now time to reveal the contents of the envelopes. If you've made it this far without getting caught, it's clear sailing the rest of the way. I ask the person who has my envelope to kindly open the flap and remove the first index card. After she removes the card, I ask her to read it aloud to the audience. She says, "December."

I then ask one of the keepers of the other envelopes to do the same. He opens the flap, pulls out the first index card, and reads it aloud: "December." Your audience will be thinking: *So, big deal—they both said December. Just a big, fat coincidence.* Perhaps. But when the person holding the third envelope opens it, pulls out the front index card, and reads, "December," the audience squirms a bit in their seats. The odds of two people both picking the same month are 1 in 12; but the odds of *three people* all choosing the same month balloons to *1 in 144.*

I then ask the person holding my envelope to remove and read the second index card aloud. "Six," announces the volunteer. The other two envelopes are opened and revealed in the same fashion, both matching the number 6 on the second index cards—much to the horror of the stunned observers. Can you see how amazing this will appear? At this point, you may want to mention that the chance of three people choosing the same date in a calendar year is 1 in 133,225 (and that's not including a leap year!). But the chance of all three people picking the same date *in the same year* would be considered mathematically impossible.

For a breathtaking conclusion, you ask the person holding your envelope to remove the final card. She announces, "1805."

You say, "The date that I chose was far from arbitrary. You see, December 6, 1805, happens to be the day that the 'Father of Modern Magic,' Jean Eugene Robert-Houdin, was born."

You ask the holders of the other two envelopes to pull out the last remaining cards and read them to the audience. In unison they say, "1805," as bedlam ensues. Your stunned and overwhelmed audience has just witnessed a miracle. And only you and your two "partners" have any idea what just happened.

What to Do If You're Busted

There are two ways to get caught. The first is if one of the two volunteers decides not to play along and says something to the effect of: "Hey! What's this? You're trying to sneak the date to me? That's cheating! You call yourself a mind reader? Get out of my house, you scoundrel!"

This horrifying scenario, thank goodness, has never happened to me. (I am referring only to the tattletale part; I've been thrown out of many houses in the past.). I find that most people are great sports and enjoy being included in the secret. Think about it: If *you* were chosen to act as a participant in this trick, would you play along or would you be like the snitch whom I just described? I rest my case. If a volunteer is selected who you suspect may not play along, you can try to influence your audience to replace him or her before starting the experiment. You can say, "I don't think you want to pick Mary. I spent a lot of time talking with her earlier. I'd hate to think that someone would suspect us of plotting this experiment."

As I mentioned, a far more likely way of getting caught is if a participant starts to laugh or acts as if he is up to something. After all, these volunteers are not expecting to receive secret instructions, and they have to do a bit of acting if they want to be convincing. If they make it obvious that they've been given special instructions, the demonstration, alas, will be ruined. But, if you like, you can minimize this risk by asking them to open their envelopes in different rooms, and then call them back in when you are ready for the conclusion. It is also important that your helpers appear to be shocked when all three dates match, which is why you added "And act surprised!" to the notes you gave them. It will be a dead giveaway if they don't seem impressed by this unfathomable coincidence.

The way I see it, you have two options if you are caught. First, you can pretend that you have to make a quick stop at the bathroom. As soon as you have a head start, run as fast as your just-been-busted-mind-reading legs will carry you. Don't stop until the sun comes up the next morning.

Or, option number two: Admit that you have indeed been caught. Say with confidence that you merely wanted to start off with a cute "trick" before getting into the real psychic feats. You then perform one of the more foolproof demonstrations in this book to restore your reputation.

And I should warn you that every once in a while a jokester will write down a different date just to ruin your trick. As long as he doesn't tell everyone about your note, the demonstration will still be effective. You can claim that not everyone possesses psychic receptors. Even if you match only one volunteer, it will still be an incredible feat.

Other Tips

 As you have just seen, the placement of the index cards in the envelopes is important for the dramatic conclusion to this exhibition. When you are giving instructions to the two volunteers, make sure you tell them to write the month on the first card, the day on the second card, and the year on the third card. And tell them to place these cards in that order in their envelopes, with the month facing out toward the flap. You can even demonstrate this to make sure they understand. And at the end of the exhibition, when the other spectators are reading the index cards aloud, you must make sure that they pull them out in that order as well. You can even ask the people reading the cards to start with the month, just to be certain they are announced in the correct order.

When the demonstration has concluded, give your "partners" some assistance in playing their roles. It is important that they act as surprised as everyone else; otherwise the audience will quickly suspect that they were somehow in on the trick. As soon as you have a moment alone with them, try to get them to promise not to reveal the answer to anyone. If you can convince them to agree, this feat will be remembered for *years* to come.

Mind reading is risky business. And sometimes a trick with a tremendous impact carries with it considerable risk. Is the effect worth the risk of getting caught? You have to decide for yourself.

*I*ndex

*A*bout the *A*uthor

ROBERT MANDELBERG is the author of two other mind-reading books *(Mystifying Mind Reading Tricks* and *Mind-Reading Card Tricks)* as well as *The Case of the Curious Campaign: A Whodunit of Many Mini-Mysteries.* He has performed comedy and magic in colleges, high schools, and nightclubs; and his play, *You're Nobody Until Somebody Kills You,* has toured nationally with the Murder on Cue Mystery Company.

Photograph by S. Keith Rosenthal

To learn more about Robert's books, performances, and latest tricks and brainteasers, visit his website at www.RobertMandelberg.com.